BL-03

W9-BLO-722

H.P. LOVECRAFT
Master of Weird Fiction

H.P. LOVECRAFT
Master of Weird Fiction

William Schoell

MORGAN REYNOLDS
Publishing, Inc.

620 South Elm Street, Suite 223
Greensboro, North Carolina 27406
http://www.morganreynolds.com

H.P. LOVECRAFT: MASTER OF WEIRD FIC

Morgan Reynolds, Inc., 620 S. Elm St., Suite 223
Greensboro, North Carolina 27406 USA

Library of Congress Cataloging-in-Publication Data

Schoell, William.
  H.P. Lovecraft : master of weird fiction / William Schoell.— 1st ed.
     v. cm. — (World writers)
Includes bibliographical references and index.
Contents: The living death — Out of the shadows — Sonia — Parkside
Avenue — The horrors of Red Hook — Creative peak — Ghostwriter — The
final years.
  ISBN 1-931798-15-X
  1. Lovecraft, H. P. (Howard Phillips), 1890-1937. 2. Horror tales,
American—History and criticism. 3. Authors, American—20th
century—Biography. [1. Lovecraft, H. P. (Howard Phillips), 1890-1937.
2. Authors, American.] I. Title. II. Series.
  PS3523.O833Z856 2004
  813'.52—dc21

                    2003010708

Printed in the United States of America
First Edition

World Writers

H.P. Lovecraft

Gwendolyn Brooks

Richard Wright

Henry Wadsworth Longfellow

Nathaniel Hawthorne

Stephen Crane

F. Scott Fitzgerald

Langston Hughes

Washington Irving

Edgar Rice Burroughs

H.G. Wells

Sir Arthur Conan Doyle

Isaac Asimov

Bram Stoker

Mary Shelley

Ida Tarbell

George Orwell

Mary Wollstonecraft

Elizabeth Cary

Marguerite Henry

Contents

H.P. Lovecraft

(Courtesy of Brown University.)

Chapter One

The Living Death

Howard Phillips Lovecraft was eighteen years old, yet he never left the house. He hardly spoke to anyone and cut himself off from human contact. He had suffered a severe nervous breakdown and desired only to be left alone to brood. He brooded over death. He brooded over loneliness. And he brooded over the nightmare fears that haunted his dreams every night. These dark things that obsessed him—death, loneliness, creatures of the night—became the basis of his weird and wonderful fiction.

Lovecraft had not always been such a dark creature. He was born in Providence, Rhode Island, on August 20, 1890. Concerning his father's side of the family he wrote, "I don't find a single mark of distinction above the mediocre country-gentry average." There were an uncommon number of clergymen among his paternal ancestors, who resided in England. When his paternal grandfather lost his fortune, he left Devonshire and sailed to New York in 1847. Lovecraft's father, Winfield Scott Lovecraft, was born in Rochester, New York. He loved the military and would have attended West Point academy had his wife, Sarah Susan Phillips Lovecraft, not objected. He was working as a traveling salesman for the Gorham Silver Company of Providence at the time of their wedding in June 1889. Winfield Scott dressed elegantly, wore a thick mustache, and spoke with such a pronounced English accent that many people mistook him for a native Englishman. His parents had urged him to keep his accent as a way to preserve his English heritage.

Sarah was the daughter of Whipple Van Buren Phillips, a successful miller who managed to buy up all the surrounding land in the village where he lived. The family experienced financial ruin in 1870, but began to recover its fortune shortly afterwards with a move to Providence, Rhode Island. By the time Lovecraft was born, his maternal grandparents were one of the most prosperous families in the area.

When Lovecraft was nearly two years of age, his parents moved to the small town of Auburndale, Massachusetts. They shared a house with a poet named Louise Imogen Guiney and her family. Many years later, Lovecraft would insist that despite his tender years, he remembered much of what he experienced at two and three years of age in Auburndale.

His yellow curly hair and friendly disposition led Louise Guiney's mother to christen young Howard "Little Sunshine," a moniker that Lovecraft and his

H.P. Lovecraft as a child, surrounded by his mother, Sarah, and his father, Winfield. *(Courtesy of Brown University.)*

friends found hilarious in later years. Lovecraft's long tresses carried an important significance for his mother, however. She had wanted a girl, and imprinted her desire on her son so strongly that as a young child he would sometimes insist, in fact, he *was* a girl. She showed him pictures of men in long hair and short pants from the eighteenth century, helping instill a romanticism for earlier ages. But Howard rebelled against the long curls, and when he was six, Sarah at last relented. She wept when his hair was cut. Curiously, at this time she also began to tell visitors her son was ugly. She avoided touching him, an aversion that probably shaped his later views about his body. Lovecraft later admitted his mother's attitudes devastated him.

At the same time, Sarah pampered and indulged her son, allowing him to eat only the food he liked the best. This did not encourage the healthiest of diets. Lovecraft became a lifelong addict of sweets and almost always declined seafood and certain vegetables. She let him choose when to get up and when to sleep. Lovecraft chose the night hours to stay awake, another habit he kept in adulthood.

Sarah also thought her son's nerves were too fragile to read fiction about the horrible or the fantastic. When he was seven, she took away his copy of H.G. Wells's *The Island of Dr. Moreau,* fearing its story of mutated man-monsters was too frightening for him.

In April 1893, Lovecraft's father suffered a stroke, apparently brought on by overwork and financial worries. Some later assumed the "paresis," or partial paralysis, that Lovecraft Sr. suffered was caused by the final stages of venereal disease. The confusion was caused by the fact that in those days the term "paresis" was often used to indicate an actual diagnosis of syphilis. In any case, Lovecraft's father had to be institutionalized. Lovecraft's parents had bought property in Auburndale so they could have their own home, but this had to be sold to pay medical bills. Lovecraft's mother was disconsolate.

The grief-stricken woman took Howard and returned to her father's home in Providence. During this period, Lovecraft's mother was so preoccupied with thoughts of her seriously ill husband that Lovecraft's grandfather "became the center of [his] entire universe." Whipple Van Buren Phillips was an extensive traveler and a highly sophisticated individual. A father substitute, Phillips fascinated young Howard with tales of his trips to Europe and his particular love for the ancient city of Rome, Italy.

In contrast, Lovecraft's maternal grandmother, Robie Phillips, was "a serene, quiet, lady" who spent most of her time trying to get the restless Howard to deport himself in a more appropriate manner. The family held a niche in the "lower-upper class" of New England, a distinction given those who had either made fortunes through hard work or kept their manners and lifestyle despite the loss of prior wealth. Young Howard learned distinctions of class that approached nobility. The best families were conservative, Anglo-Saxon, and devoted to the values of capitalism. They revered English and Northern European traditions. Sobriety, thrift, and hard work could earn a person respect, provided he or she possessed the proper background. Recent immigrants, including Jews, Italians, Irish, and Portuguese, found no easy path to respectability in this rigidly class-conscious world.

There were also two aunts in the Phillips's household. The older of the two, Lillian, helped ignite Lovecraft's passion for literature and chemistry. Annie possessed a high-spirited personality that lightened the often somber atmosphere in the home. Howard would do imitations of her friends when they came to call. Both women eventually married and left the family manor. In later years, when they were either divorced or widowed, they again became quite close to their nephew.

Lovecraft claimed he was able to read by age four. If he saw a word whose meaning he did not know, he would run to the dictionary. The Lovecraft family had an extensive library that had been brought over from England; these books were given to Howard after his father was institutionalized. Howard spent many hours poring over the family books; he especially loved *Grimm's Fairy Tales.*

In January of 1896, another tragedy struck when Howard's grandmother became ill and died. The family observed a morbidly strict regimen of mourning. Lovecraft's mother and aunts wore black around the clock, which he found disturbing and depressing. When their backs were turned, Howard would pin scraps of colored paper to the women's dark outfits. Because of this, they would have to carefully check their garments before they stepped out of the house. His mother discontinued wearing her mourning clothes when she realized they worried Howard.

The gloominess of the household gave Lovecraft nightmares in which he was visited by strange creatures that he referred to as "night-gaunts." These frightening beings would whisk him at unimaginable speeds through space and attack him with pitchforks. He became so disturbed at the thought of encountering them in his dreams that he would struggle to stay awake half the night. In the morning, he would try to sketch the creatures that had pursued him. Lovecraft credited an illustrated edition of *Paradise Lost* with generating some of these night-gaunts, but most of them were from his vivid imagination. Later, many of these strange beings would inhabit his scariest stories.

By the age of six and seven, Lovecraft spent so much time with his elders that he had no friends his own age, nor did he want any. Other children saw him as unlikable and superior. Lovecraft was more interested in reading and dreaming than in running around with what he saw as infantile playmates. His disinterest in physical activity during this period was so intense he even refused to attend a dance class his mother thought he might enjoy.

He did, however, take violin lessons after pleading with her to buy him an instrument at age seven. His habit of whistling melodies and rhythmically thumping his feet in time with the music suggested to his family that he might be musically inclined. At first he took to his lessons with some diligence, but after awhile, he grew tired of the practicing. He played a Mozart piece at a recital when he was nine, but discontinued his lessons thereafter. To get out of the lessons, Lovecraft enlisted the help of the family doctor, who suggested his continuing might be injurious to Lovecraft's delicate nervous disposition.

Lovecraft lived most of his childhood in his grandparents' Victorian mansion on Angell Street in Providence, Rhode Island. *(Courtesy of Brown University.)*

One activity Lovecraft enjoyed as a child was playing in the lot next to his home on Angell Street. A handyman who worked for the family built Howard a crude playhouse on the lot. Lovecraft, who was fascinated with trains, imagined his playhouse was a vast terminal and roundhouse. Boxes and wheelbarrows were turned into engines and cars, and from the roof of this "engine house," as it came to be called, Lovecraft would direct his imaginary trains to go in any direction he chose.

By the age of eight, Lovecraft had progressed from *Grimm's Fairy Tales* to *Bulfinch's Mythology*. He loved the tales of Greek gods, monsters, and ordinary mortals caught up by the fates. However, he noted, "I never had the slightest shadow of belief in the supernatural." Neither was Lovecraft particularly religious. His love of stories about old gods and cosmic menaces did not mean that he actually believed in such entities himself.

At seven and eight, Lovecraft began writing poetry—his first poem was about Ulysses—and short stories. By the time he was nine, he had written enough poems to collect them in a volume for his mother. The subject of these poems ranged from the Moon to his grandfather's beloved Rome to paganism.

When he was eight years old, Lovecraft was sent to elementary school. Previously, his family had been afraid he was too high-strung and sensitive to sit still and obey the teacher. Lovecraft claimed he knew more than the rest of the students through his reading. Aside from making a couple of friends, he found the instruction "useless;" he was taken out of school and not sent back until four years had passed. Lovecraft's father, still institutionalized, died during this time. It was much more traumatic for his mother than for Howard, who barely remembered the man.

At age nine, he took a serious interest in chemistry. This was in part because of his Aunt Lillian, who loved scientific matters, and partly because of a family friend who had written a chemistry primer for beginners. Armed with a copy of the book, Lovecraft would sequester himself in the cellar, where he set up a simple laboratory. His grandfather encouraged his interest by buying him supplies and equipment. Although no great chemical compounds resulted from this experimentation, the precocious child put out a daily paper of his "findings" called *The Scientific Gazette*. This was only the beginning of his interest in privately published newsletters and "the small press."

At ten, having read of the Borchgrevink expedition to the South Pole, which was the first to spend a winter in the Antarctic, Lovecraft developed a lifelong fascination with the exploration of this frozen area. He wrote Antarctic stories as a child, but these were forgettable, amateurish efforts. For a while he became so interested in science of all kinds, as well as geography and history, that he forgot about writing and even neglected his reading. At twelve, when he re-entered school, he developed a fascination for astronomy, which for a while pushed aside all of his other interests. "This pursuit of science gave me something of a contempt for art and literature," he wrote.

At the age of ten, Lovecraft began a lifelong fascination with the Antarctic.
(Courtesy of the Library of Congress.)

This "contempt" did not last long. He soon became addicted to the Sherlock Holmes detective stories written by Sir Arthur Conan Doyle. The oppressive atmosphere in his home also led to his doing something he had never done before—seeking out friendships with the other boys and girls with whom he now attended school. With these youngsters he formed the P.D.A., or Providence Detective Agency. Lovecraft and his friends would go about the neighborhood pretending to spot and investigate crimes. Since they did not witness real crimes, the members of the P.D.A. would invent them. Many an afternoon, Lovecraft would set his mind to the task of creating fake bloodstains that might even fool his fellow "detectives."

He also had these friends over to his "engine house," where they would help him mastermind the running of his numerous train lines. They formed a "Slater Avenue Army" and even built an elaborate fort out of earth and rocks. When not playing soldier or "railway" or hunting down dastardly murderers, Lovecraft and his chums explored the nearby woods or played other games of make-believe. Even by himself, Lovecraft loved to explore the streets of Providence, enjoying the atmosphere of the old Victorian houses and studying the architecture. On rainy evenings he swore he could almost see the ghosts of the long-ago past shimmering in the pools of light cast by the gas lamps on the wet, cobblestone streets. Everything about the past fascinated Lovecraft, and he often wished he had been born many decades— or even a century or more—earlier.

Before his early teens, Lovecraft developed another interest that made good use of his vivid imagination. Using dirt and clay, as well as wooden strips and pieces of cardboard, Howard would construct miniature villages on tabletops. He would then concoct elaborate stories about the village's inhabitants. He was not overly concerned with scale—a backyard shed might be larger than the town's church, for instance—as long as the basic design or layout of the town was recognizable. Tin tracks for his beloved trains would complete the assembly. Some of these toy villages became quite large and intricate. "There was a kind of intoxication in being lord of a visible world (albeit a miniature one) and determining the flow of its events," he remembered. He also constructed a toy theater with cardboard scenery and chose the appropriate actors from among his toys.

In addition to Sherlock Holmes stories, Lovecraft became addicted to the fantastic Nick Carter detective tales, as well as the rags-to-riches novels of Horatio

Alger. Eventually, he discovered the work of Edgar Allan Poe. Poe's macabre genius and dark view of the world struck a resonating chord in Lovecraft. The incredible monsters and high adventure of the Arabian Nights stories were also early influences.

Although Lovecraft was considered a sensitive, even sickly, child, he was able to stand up for himself. His temper often led him into fisticuffs with other boys. Lovecraft claimed he was too skinny and weak to win many of these fights unless he acted so fiercely crazy that the other boy would run for his life in sheer fright. At fourteen, he developed an aptitude for shooting .22-caliber rifles with a fair amount of accuracy, although he later became "hypersensitive" to loud sounds. He was equally sensitive to bad odors and hated being in crowds.

He did rather well at school, although his teacher thought he was too undisciplined and much too inclined to contradict her. It was only his obvious intelligence and good grades that kept the woman from losing all patience with him. He took special joy in arguing with her during history class. As she was a "Yankee," Lovecraft and some of his friends would feign more sympathy with the Confederacy than they actually felt.

Lovecraft firmly informed the teacher that he would not give a speech at graduation, even though it was the custom for each student to do so. At the last minute, however, he quickly scribbled a speech during the graduation exercises. After the other students were through, Lovecraft took to the platform and in extremely conde-

The works of Edgar Allan Poe were an early influence on the writings of H.P. Lovecraft. *(Courtesy of the Library of Congress.)*

scending tones gave a stern and haughty lecture on the works of astronomer Sir William Herschel. He used as many "big" words as he knew in order to sound as intellectually superior as possible. The audience was charmed by the boy, however, and gave him a hearty round of applause.

This triumph at graduation was followed by disaster. In early 1904, a crisis in the Phillips's family business occurred. Lovecraft's grandfather was the president of the Owyhee Corporation, which oversaw the irrigation of property adjacent to the Snake River in Idaho. When a dam on the river burst, it badly affected the business—and the old man's health. Whipple Phillips directed the construction of a second dam, but it too collapsed. The two consecutive fiascoes set the Owyhee Corporation teetering on the brink of bankruptcy. Then, while visiting a friend, Grandfather Phillips suffered what was termed a "paralytic shock." He died the following day, on March 27, 1904. Whipple's death, combined with the blows to his company, greatly reduced the family's fortunes. Lovecraft was devastated by the death of the only real father he had ever known. And there was more bad news: the Victorian mansion in which they resided had to be sold.

This was a shocking development for Lovecraft. He was losing the only home he had ever known, as well as his beloved lot beside the house where he had built his tiny towns, railway, and fort. "I felt I had lost my entire adjustment to the cosmos," remembered Lovecraft, "for what indeed was HPL [Howard Phillips Lovecraft] without the remembered rooms and hallways and hangings and cherry trees and fountain and ivy-grown arch and stable and gardens and all the rest?"

Lovecraft and his mother were forced to move into a five-room apartment with an attic, also located on Angell Street. It was only a few blocks from the mansion, but it might as well have been a universe away. Next door was a vacant lot that Lovecraft used as a playground, but it only reminded him of the far superior "engine house" at the family mansion.

The new apartment seemed stuffy and confining; it stifled his imagination. He missed his doting grandfather and the way the old man and the servants would fuss over him. Life seemed intolerable and boring and hopeless. Lovecraft contemplated suicide and decided the easiest thing would be to drown himself in the Barrington River. "And yet certain elements—notably scientific curiosity and a sense of world drama—held me back," he later wrote.

Lovecraft shed much of his depression by attending high school in the fall, where he was fascinated by physics and how it challenged his former views of the cosmos. He studied the ancient civilizations and lost cultures of the Minoans and the Byzantine Empire, and was swept up into the world of archaeology and its historical findings. He was also intrigued by real-life mysteries, such as the giant statues on Easter Island.

He also began writing again, stories such as "The Beast in the Cave," which he composed at age fifteen. The story concerns a nearly hysterical man who is lost in a deep cavern with what he fears is a dangerous animal. He kills the beast, only to discover it was really another man. While nowhere near the level of his greatest stories, "The Beast in the Cave" certainly demonstrates Lovecraft's writing talent at an early age.

In addition to fiction, Lovecraft began submitting articles on astronomy to the *Providence Tribune*, as well as local papers in smaller towns. One of the latter periodicals published his essay entitled "Can the Moon Be Reached by Man?" Asked to submit an essay for an English class, he used the same piece he had written for the journal. The next day his English teacher accused him of plagiarism. She was sure she had read the same piece or something similar in a magazine. "You certainly have," Lovecraft assured her, whipping out a clipping of his original article.

Lovecraft got along with all of his high school teachers, except for the man who taught algebra. Lovecraft felt he should get credit for coming up with the right answer even if his method varied from the one taught by the instructor. Despite his ingenuity, Lovecraft did not do well in and did not enjoy mathematics. He realized a career in astronomy was therefore out of the question, as it was a science thoroughly grounded in mathematics. He would have to pursue another profession. It crossed his mind to become a chemist, as he still enjoyed fiddling in the high school's science lab.

Later in his life, Lovecraft wrote hundreds of letters to fellow authors and admirers about all aspects of his life and work but said very little about the nervous breakdown he suffered beginning in his final year of high school and lasting for five years. He had planned to go to Brown University in Providence after graduation, but those plans had to be curtailed after his emotional collapse. His failure to get a college degree was a great source of embarrassment to him and negatively affected his job prospects—and indeed his entire life.

Lovecraft had always been sensitive, but what was it that drove him so deep into depression that he could not function? Why did he stay home behind closed doors and dark curtains and not interact with anyone but his mother? His age at the time—the problems began when he was around seventeen—may provide a clue. For one thing, his growing body began to bear out his mother Sarah's bleak assessment of his physical attributes. As a small child, Lovecraft was cute enough to be called "Little Sunshine," but as a young man reaching adulthood, his looks were a different story. After puberty, his features began to elongate, and he became a homely teenager with a long, bony, cadaverous face—a face that did not attract the opposite sex. It was upsetting to him that his appearance was so ungainly.

Many people who do not possess a handsome appearance cultivate a charming personality, outgoing manner, or physical skill that makes up for their lack of beauty. Lovecraft eventually did the same, but at eighteen his continued depression over his family's reduced circumstances prevented this adjustment. There may have been other problems that he kept to himself. As a young man, he would have, for the first time in a mature fashion, contemplated his father's tragic fate. He might have wondered if the same future were in store for him. He would have mourned his grandfather and the loss of everything the old man represented—the genteel lifestyle and the hope of an inheritance and continued prosperity throughout his life. Combined with his sensitive, introspective nature and his fears for the future, his gloom over his present state could easily have driven him over the edge.

Howard Phillips Lovecraft, at the age of eighteen, did not look upon the world with optimism. It might even be said he was dead to the world.

Chapter Two

Out of the Shadows

"I could hardly bear to see or speak to anyone, and liked to shut out the world by pulling down dark shades and using artificial light." So did Lovecraft remember the period during his nervous breakdown, when he spent most of his time at home behind closed doors and spoke to hardly anyone besides his mother. Now and then he might speak to one of his aunts, but on most occasions he found it difficult to communicate. The depression he felt was so all-encompassing he lacked the energy to do simple tasks. He remained in this state for over five years, until he was in his early twenties, and it left him feeling that he would always be a freak. As horrible as the experience was, though, it might have confirmed a deep need Lovecraft had to feel different than other people. Maybe he suffered because he was not like the average person. It was the price he had to pay to be different.

The depression made it impossible for him to go to

college. Even after this dark period was over, he could not bring himself to go to Brown University for any purpose, even to enter the library or the observatory. He shunned the company of friends he had known before the breakdown, those who had attended university and gone on to have careers. "I simply prefer to have intimacy with those who have never known me, save at my worst," he later wrote. He was quite heartbroken that he never got to know Brown as a student would know it. Therefore, he cut Brown, and what the school reminded him of, out of his life.

Slowly, when he was twenty-three, Lovecraft began to draw out of his death-like state. To combat boredom, he began reading popular magazines of the period. One of his favorites was *The Argosy*, one of three adventure magazines in a chain published by Frank A. Munsey. Munsey also published *All-Story Magazine* and *The Cavalier*. These magazines provided escapist fantasies for mostly male readers, in a time when almost universal literacy was a relatively new phenomenon in America. As such, they were precursors to the cheaply printed "pulp magazines" that became popular in the 1920s and 1930s. They occasionally carried weird fiction of the kind Lovecraft liked best. For example, *All-Story* published one of the first story series on travels to Mars, and the original tales of the jungle-dwelling English hero Tarzan, both written by fantasist Edgar Rice Burroughs.

One day, Lovecraft read a story in *The Argosy* that so irritated him he sat down and drafted a letter to the

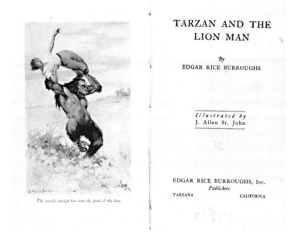

TARZAN AND THE
LION MAN

By
EDGAR RICE BURROUGHS

Illustrated by
J. Allen St. John

EDGAR RICE BURROUGHS, Inc.
Publishers
TARZANA   CALIFORNIA

Edgar Rice Burroughs's tales of life on Mars, as well as the exploits of Tarzan, were favorites of Lovecraft's. *(Courtesy of the Library of Congress.)*

editor expressing his contempt. The letter was written in a style that satirized the writer whose work he had found so objectionable. Other readers sent in letters objecting to Lovecraft's satire, and before long, the whole letter column was devoted to the controversy. The editor of *The Argosy* noted that even long-time readers were afraid the hysteria over Lovecraft would crowd out all other comments. Lovecraft and one letter writer who vehemently disagreed with him decided to end the whole business by jointly composing a poem that appeared in the October 1914 issue of the magazine. Lovecraft claimed he never again read another issue of *The Argosy*.

The letters in *The Argosy* brought Lovecraft to the attention of the United Amateur Press Association (UAPA), a nationwide organization of amateur writers who wrote and published their own magazines. The president of UAPA invited Lovecraft to join. After becoming a member, Lovecraft composed a recruiting pamphlet for the organization in 1915. In this pamphlet, he explained the word "amateur" in this case did not describe someone who was incapable of professional standards; indeed some members of the association were journalists by trade. Rather, the members of the group were simply disinterested in the commercial aspects of journalism, at least as far as their UAPA activities were concerned.

"The atmosphere is wholly fraternal," wrote Lovecraft, "and courtesy takes the place of currency." Not only did the group provide training for those amateur members who wished to become professionals, it also encouraged intellectual stimulation for all kinds of people regardless of their age, sex, or background. Some members of the group put out small-circulation magazines or journals at their own expense; the other members were invited to contribute material to these periodicals, which covered numerous subjects and often resembled high school or college newspapers. (Today these small magazines and publishers are collectively known as the "small press.")

Lovecraft made so many friends and found such intellectual satisfaction from involvement in the United Amateur Press Association that he regretted not learning of the organization many years earlier. He threw himself into communicating with the other members and contributing articles and stories to the various publications. The UAPA provided a lifeline for Lovecraft, something with which he could pull himself out of his depressed state and back into a kind of normalcy. "I obtained a renewed will to live," he wrote, "and found a sphere in which I could feel that my efforts were not wholly futile."

That same year, Lovecraft was appointed chairman of the Department of Public Criticism of the UAPA. He believed there was little point in praising someone's efforts just because of his or her standing in the organization, and decided to be blunt with his criticism. In his opinion, it was the only way for the UAPA to maintain a certain standard. To take the sting out of his critical remarks, Lovecraft offered to critique—and even revise—free of charge any article or story that the author cared to send him. (He continued to do free revisions for many years.)

There were two reactions to this suggestion. He was swamped with material from fellow members who anxiously wished him to make their work more acceptable, and he received many angry letters from members who resented his criticism and found his offer to "fix" their work condescending and obnoxious. It is likely that more members applauded his efforts than vilified them, because the following year he was appointed vice president of the UAPA, and in 1917, he became president.

From 1915 to 1919, Lovecraft also put out his own paper, *The Conservative*. It was his medium for decrying what he saw as the decline in literary and grammatical standards in recent years. In addition to literary criticism, he solicited articles that would conform to his

H.P. Lovecraft in his twenties.
(Courtesy of Brown University.)

favorite causes and world-view. Lovecraft and *The Conservative* abhorred the use of liquor and were in favor of prohibition—making the consumption of alcoholic beverages illegal. In addition, the editorial policy was militaristic, patriotic, and stridently opposed to anyone who preached pacifism. *The Conservative* also supported the ascendancy of English and other Caucasian races over "lesser divisions of mankind" and a capitalistic government over one devoted to socialism, or anarchy. These were causes that were held in high regard by a great many Americans at that time.

Lovecraft's paper began publication at an opportune time for those who held such opinions. World War I had broken out the year before, when, on June 28, 1914, a Serbian terrorist assassinated Archduke Francis Ferdinand of Austria-Hungary in Sarajevo, Bosnia.

Serbian nationalists carried out the assassination as part of their dream of establishing a Serbian state. The deeper origins of the war were complicated, and stretched back several decades. By the end of August 1914, many of the nations of Europe had joined the war, either on the side of the Allies—Britain, France, and Russia, or with Austria and Germany. People on both sides of the Atlantic had been expecting war to erupt for years. At first, the United States was determined to stay out of the conflict, but when Germany began a submarine campaign against the United States because of its aid to the British, President Woodrow Wilson declared America at war on the side of the Allies in 1917.

Lovecraft fervently supported the war. The only aspect of it that dismayed him was that the "Teutonic" peoples of Britain and Germany were pitted against one another. The word "Aryans" would later replace "Teutons" in his diatribes. Both words referred to Northern Europeans, whom Lovecraft considered superior to all other groups of humanity.

"Englishmen and Germans are blood brothers, descended from the same stern Woden-worshipping ancestors, blessed with the same rugged virtues, and fired with the same noble ambitions," Lovecraft wrote in an editorial. "In a world of diverse and hostile races the joint mission of these virile men is one of union and co-operation with their fellow Teutons in the defense of civilization against the onslaughts of all others."

Although it was a handy soapbox for his views,

Lovecraft decided to discontinue *The Conservative* when he was made official editor of the UAPA newsletter in 1920. He was frustrated, however, in his new position. He wanted to put out a paper he could be proud of, but few of the submissions met his standards. He was also discouraged by his involvement in a local group known as the Providence Amateur Press Club. Most of the members were poorly-educated Irish immigrants who attended high school night classes and worked by day. Lovecraft admired their desire to better themselves and offered to help them, but he felt no true connection to them. They came from sections of Providence that were very different from Angell Street, and they took too

President Woodrow Wilson *(third from left)* came to the aid of the Allies in 1917 with the United States' entry into World War I. *(Courtesy of the Library of Congress.)*

long to prepare work for Lovecraft to review, if they did so at all. The club managed to put out two editions of the *Providence Amateur* around 1915, but disbanded after a year.

Lovecraft had problems with some of the officers of the *Providence Amateur* group, as well. He described the president, Victor Basinet, as being a dangerous socialist and labor agitator, but hoped Victor's native intelligence would straighten out his ideas. The editor, John Dunn, so hated England and all it stood for that he supported the Germans. This led to his being arrested and sent to federal prison for twenty years. "I am done with Dunn!" declared Lovecraft.

Lovecraft grew frustrated at having to sit out the war while other men his age became soldiers. In early 1917, he went to the recruiting station of the Rhode Island National Guard where he hoped to enlist. Lovecraft did not inform his mother of his plans. Without a husband to care for, she had transferred her smothering, almost desperate, attentions to her only child. When she found out that he had become a private in the Ninth Coast Artillery, she was horrified. She could not bear the thought of losing a son as well as a husband, and was convinced Lovecraft's delicate nature would practically ensure his destruction.

Mrs. Lovecraft took immediate action. She went to the family physician and asked him to contact the military on her son's behalf. When examined by the army surgeon, Lovecraft had managed to suppress the facts of his nervous breakdown, sensitive disposition, and assorted psychosomatic ailments. The family physician, however, told the surgeon all about Lovecraft's emotional and physical problems. With patriotic fever at a high pitch, ensuring plenty of enlistees, the army could afford to reject thousands of men for medical reasons. The family doctor's report was more than enough to get Lovecraft's enlistment annulled.

Lovecraft was humiliated. The army rarely reversed its decisions once they had accepted a recruit. The surgeon declared it "most irregular" for them to change their minds and reject Lovecraft, who was now mortified every time he saw a khaki-clad soldier. He would always wonder if the experience of being in the army would have "killed or cured" him.

Lovecraft may have complained of his mother's suffocating influence on his life, but it is clear from his letters that he often allowed himself to be coddled by her—and by his doctor. Lovecraft claimed it was his physician who convinced him to accept classification as "Class V, Division G"—"totally and permanently unfit"—for the draft. "It is not flattering to be reminded of my utter uselessness twice within the space of six months," he wrote, "but the war is a great exposer of human failings and inefficiency." According to Lovecraft, the family doctor felt he was not only unfit for combat, but also for "any work requiring discipline and schedule." Supposedly, he would never be able to tolerate having a job or doing much of anything that took him away from the comforts of home. While he said this was the opinion of the family doctor, it is also probably true that he had become too used to being watched after by his well-meaning, but suffocating, mother on Angell Street.

Although his activities with the UAPA often left him little time to compose fiction, he did manage to write a few stories during this period. He took a stroll with his aunt through the Swan Point cemetery in 1917 and noticed a tombstone from 1711 with a skull and crossbones upon its face. This inspired him to write his first short story in nine years, "The Tomb," a fascinating study of a lonely and morbid mind and its obsession with the comfort of death. As Lovecraft had contemplated suicide, and would do so again, this theme was familiar. "Dagon" (1917), "Polaris" (1917), and "Psychopompos" (1918) were also written during the war years.

According to Robert Bloch, who was later a protégé of Lovecraft's, his mentor's writing got better with the passing years. "In earlier tales he often relied on the excessive use of adjectives rather than the power of suggestion, with disastrous results," wrote Bloch. "But gradually he learned the value of restraint and of a more realistic approach. Refining his style, he also refined his methods." To modern readers, Lovecraft's prose is somewhat overwritten, quaint, and almost Victorian. Yet it still has the power to grip, frighten, and fascinate.

Lovecraft communicated with W. Paul Cook, who was also a fiction writer and publisher of an amateur journal entitled *Monadnock Monthly*, among others. He

The writings of Lord Dunsany were a major influence on Lovecraft's work. *(Courtesy of the Library of Congress.)*

admired Cook's writing and sent him "The Tomb"— with some trepidation. Cook loved the story and promised to print it. When the publisher paid a call on Lovecraft in Providence, the latter observed "some little rusticities and plebeianisms in his dress and demeanor." Ever the snob, Lovecraft noted that after the visit, "I lost some of my awe for his fictional greatness."

Around this time, Lovecraft discovered Irish fantasy writer Lord Dunsany, and became as fascinated by his work as he had been by Poe's. An acquaintance had recommended Dunsany because he felt Lovecraft's story "Polaris" bore similarities to the work of Dunsany. He eventually counted Dunsany as a major influence on stories such as "The White Ship" (1919) and "The Doom that Came to Sarnath" (1919).

In October 1919, Lovecraft went to the Copley-Plaza Hotel in Boston to hear Dunsany, who lectured on his working methods and read one of his short plays, "The Queen's Enemies." Lovecraft was very favorably impressed with the author but did not ask for his autograph, as he hated fawning over important people. Other writers of the macabre that he admired were Arthur Machen, Algernon Blackwood, M.R. James, and of course, Poe.

As she grew older, Lovecraft's mother developed severe emotional problems. Much of this had to do with the deaths of her husband and father, and her reduced circumstances brought about by their deaths. Whenever his mother had a mental "episode," he would also spiral downward into a twilight world of solitude and despair. At these times, it was impossible for him to write. During his mother's first breakdown and hospitalization, he could only attend to his UAPA duties by rote.

Sarah Lovecraft's health took a turn for the worse during the war. She suffered frequent attacks of hysteria and depression. She briefly moved in with Lovecraft's older aunt, Lillian, while his younger aunt, Annie, moved in with him and tried to care for him. Lovecraft missed his mother so much, and was so worried about her illness, that he could hardly eat or write. The nervous strain eventually made him dizzy, gave him severe headaches, and blurred his vision. His mother's physical symptoms, such as stomachaches, were thought to be psychosomatic in nature. That did not stop Lovecraft from deluding himself at times into thinking a change of diet might bring improvement.

His mother wrote to Lovecraft every day and did her best to put on a good front for her son's sake. When there was no improvement in her health, she was hospitalized for a time. She remained optimistic, at least in her letters to her son, but the treatment proved futile. In March of 1919, she was moved to the Butler Hospital for the Insane. Ironically, this was the same institution where Lovecraft's father had died twenty-one years before. While Lovecraft was pleased she was getting the best of care and desperately hoped for a change for the better, he was miserable over his mother's long absence. He could barely eat and complained that his writing brought on blurred vision and headaches.

Sarah remained in the sanitarium for two years. Lovecraft wrote her long letters and visited regularly. They walked through the well-kept grounds of an area called "The Grotto," through the Butler Woods overlooking the Seekonk River. Curiously, hospital records show Lovecraft never entered the sanitarium building. Lovecraft's characters, like those of Poe, were often people who had gone mad. Several of his later stories would center on men confined to mental institutions, but he had no desire to see the interior of one for himself.

On May 24, 1921, Lovecraft's mother died while undergoing a gall bladder operation. He was completely devastated. He was not, however, entirely unprepared and claimed in letters to friends that, in spite of his distress, he did not weep or carry on, as that would be "emotional" and "vulgar." At a time like this, when he felt small, bereft, lonely—and motherless—Lovecraft needed more than ever to feel superior to others.

Despite his attempt at bravado, he was in terrible agony. The one person who loved him unconditionally was gone. He had loved to talk things over with her and to hear her opinions. She was the "nucleus" of his existence, someone he admired without reservation.

Lovecraft thought of suicide frequently during his mother's long illness, but knew his death would be too much for her to bear. Now that she was dead, there was nothing to hold him back. He realized, however, suicide would only forever cut him off from the great adventure that was life.

Deeply depressed, he lost interest in his writing, the works of Poe and Dunsany, the UAPA, and even his correspondence for a time. After awhile, his aunts and amateur journalism brought him out of his misery. He would sit around in bathrobe and slippers writing copiously as his aunts urged him to get dressed and get out of the house. Eventually, they convinced him to travel to New Hampshire to meet with a fellow UAPA member who had started writing professionally. This reignited his creative instincts and his desire to meet and be with other people of like minds.

One of these like-minded people was a woman who would change Lovecraft's life in a way that neither he nor anyone who knew him would have thought was possible.

Chapter Three

Sonia

Sonia H. Greene, a Russian-Jewish immigrant Lovecraft met through amateur journalism, became the second most important woman in his life. The two met in July 1921, at a small press convention held at the Brunswick Hotel in Boston. It was not love at first sight, but more a meeting and, eventually, a melding of two harmonious minds and spirits. For a brief time, Sonia published her own amateur journal called *The Rainbow*, and Lovecraft worked with her on a horror tale published as "The Invisible Monster."

It was not long after they met that Sonia began to visit Lovecraft in Providence. She would stay at a local inn, the Crown Hotel, and phone Lovecraft when she arrived. On her first visit, Sonia was introduced to Lovecraft's elder aunt, Lillian, who was very impressed by her. She caused Aunt Lillian to raise her opinion of amateur journalism and Lovecraft's participation in it. After showing her where he lived, Lovecraft proudly took Sonia on a tour of Providence. In the evening, they attended a concert at Roger Williams Park. Lovecraft noted Sonia was not opposed to spending money and treated them to a ride in a "horseless" coach. "If she is determined to blow de coin," he wrote, "it ain't no business of mine to stop her!"

The next day, Sonia took both Lovecraft and Lillian to lunch at the Crown Hotel. "Mme. Greene is certainly a person of the most admirable qualities," Lovecraft wrote, "whose generous and kindly cast of mind is by no means feigned, and whose intelligence and devotion to art merit the sincerest approbation. The volatility incidental to a Continental and non-Ayran heritage should not blind the analytical observer to the solid work and genuine cultivation which underlie it." In other words, Lovecraft was willing to overlook the fact that the generous Sonia was both a foreigner and a Jew.

On a subsequent trip to Providence, Sonia was introduced to Lovecraft's younger aunt, now Mrs. Annie Gamwell, and the two hit it off immediately. Sonia even wanted Lovecraft's aunt to come and live with her in New York, as Annie was separated from her husband. Sonia thought the city might suit her during such a difficult time. Sonia got along so well with the two aunts that Lovecraft even became a little jealous, particularly when the three women sat and discussed matters that did not interest him, which was just about anything but literature, culture, or history.

On one trip, Sonia and Lovecraft somehow missed each other at the Providence train depot. Sonia took a cab to his house, found he was not there, and then rode back to the train station. Finally, the two found each other and had lunch at the Crown. After a lengthy afternoon visit, Lovecraft was walking Sonia back to the depot when a downpour began. Lovecraft had a bizarre aversion to umbrellas, so the two were thoroughly drenched by the time they arrived at the depot. Sonia wanted to give Lovecraft money to pay for a taxi back to his house, but he refused. He said he and his clothing were so soaked through that he could hardly get any wetter. Lovecraft would on occasion decline Sonia's generous gestures, but it did not escape his notice that she apparently had plenty of money.

Lovecraft might well have envied such prosperity,

Sonia Greene provided Lovecraft with both financial and emotional support. *(Courtesy of Brown University.)*

for he rarely had a dollar to spend on luxuries. Part of the reason for his poverty came from his being taught to perceive himself as a New England "gentleman." Families of the upper classes often looked more favorably on people who maintained a facade of wealth, despite the loss of it, than those who stooped to labor for income. Moreover, Lovecraft's education had provided no instruction in any practical skills that might lead to employment. In the early 1920s, according to Lovecraft, he and his two aunts shared an inheritance of twenty thousand dollars. They doled out a sum of fifteen dollars a week to Lovecraft. He would later supplement his allowance by earning small fees from selling his stories, but his most profitable life's work would come as a ghostwriter and rewrite man for other authors.

Lovecraft's chances for advancement as a writer might have improved in New York, especially given its status as the capital of American publishing, but he resisted Sonia's suggestions that he visit the city. He found the prospect daunting. Although he had been to Boston, New York was much larger and more intimidating. He was also afraid his presence might be too much of an imposition on Sonia, who promised to pay all of his expenses.

Sonia and Lovecraft had many acquaintances in common, among them the poet and dramatist Samuel E. Loveman. Lovecraft had admired Loveman's poetry and sent a letter to his last known address, inquiring as to whether or not the man was still among the living. Amused, Loveman wrote back that yes, he was still alive, if not by much. Loveman needed a job, and Sonia suggested he come to New York where he might more easily find employment. When Loveman failed to find work, Sonia decided to cheer up the discouraged man by having him talk to Lovecraft over the telephone. Loveman told Lovecraft he would stay in New York only if Lovecraft himself came to visit. On a sudden impulse, Lovecraft decided to go to the city. He was anxious to meet another of his literary heroes. It was early April 1922.

Lovecraft caught the train to New York the next morning and spent the ride reading stories by Lord Dunsany. He was impressed by his first sight of the skyscrapers of Manhattan, which he spotted from the Harlem River viaduct. Again, there was a misadventure involving trains. In the vastness of Pennsylvania Station, Sonia

Lovecraft was initially fascinated by the sites in Manhattan.
(Courtesy of the Library of Congress.)

and Loveman missed Lovecraft. The eternally pessimistic Loveman went back to Brooklyn, where he was staying with Sonia. Sonia, however, finally located Lovecraft, and the two caught up with Loveman just as he was climbing the steps at Sonia's address, 259 Parkside Avenue. This street is located in Flatbush, a neighborhood in Brooklyn.

Sonia let the two men share her apartment while she boarded with a neighbor. The following day, Lovecraft began to explore the city. He and Loveman spent most of the day at the Metropolitan Museum of Art, where they explored an ancient Egyptian tomb that had been moved and rebuilt block by block. Lovecraft looked with fascination at the actual, uncovered face of a mummified priest from 2700 B.C. He particularly marveled at any statue or exhibit that reminded him of ancient Rome. Lovecraft held a lifelong fascination with empires, from those of Greece and Rome to the one British King George III ruled at the time of the American Revolution.

Their next stop was the office of George Julian Houtain on lower Broadway. Houtain and his wife, Dorothy, were publishers of a (mostly) humorous magazine entitled *Home Brew*. Lovecraft had submitted two long, serialized stories to them—*Herbert West: Reanimator* and *The Lurking Fear*. Houtain gave him copies of the latest issue, which contained his work. Lovecraft delighted in picking up copies at the news-stand and showing his byline off to his friends. "Reg'lar author 'n' ever'thin'," he wrote at the time.

Herbert West: Reanimator, which was to become one of Lovecraft's most famous stories, was serialized during 1921 and 1922. It related the adventures of the title character and his unnamed friend and assistant—the narrator—who is as fascinated by West as he is appalled. This man is "dragged into" the horrors that evolve as West is determined to discover a formula that will bring dead tissue back to life. First, he tries to revivify dead animals, but soon begins working on humans. One complication is that he needs bodies, lots of bodies, to use in experiments.

The story starts as a more lurid variation of *Frankenstein*, but soon takes its own path as West tries more daring ways to come by the fresh specimens—the newly dead—he needs. Trying his formula on his enemy, the recently deceased dean of the medical school, he succeeds in bringing the man back to life—but only as an insane, gibbering ghoul. He next joins the army as a doctor during World War I so he can have access to dead soldiers. His original goal of conquering death is virtually forgotten as he experiments more out of morbid curiosity than for any noble purpose.

Gruesome and fast-paced (despite the slow opening paragraphs of each segment, which were originally meant to recap the previous serialized chapter for the magazine's readers), *Herbert West: Reanimator* is great fun—if atypical Lovecraft. The story's energetic ghoulishness is compelling, but Lovecraft saw it only as cheap commercial writing. Maybe because he did not take it as seriously as most of his other work, some of the best sections border on black comedy.

The Lurking Fear (1922), which Lovecraft also later claimed to not like, concerns a mysterious, unseen creature decimating humans in the vicinity of an abandoned mansion on top of a mountain. Every time there is a thunderstorm, people disappear or are dismembered. Lovecraft incorporated "cheap" but effective shock scenes in this story—also atypical for him. At one point, the narrator wonders why a colleague of his has been silently staring out a window for so long. When he goes to his side, he discovers the front half of his head, his entire face, has been nibbled away. Again, although Lovecraft disparaged the story as one of his weaker efforts, *The Lurking Fear* is highly suspenseful and creepy.

Lovecraft enjoyed exploring Brooklyn. He greatly admired Montague Street, in Brooklyn Heights, which reminded him a bit of the Back Bay district of Boston. A view of the New York skyline from the Manhattan Bridge elicited this passage in a letter, in which Lovecraft deliberately imitated the style of Lord Dunsany: "Out of the waters it rose at twilight; cold, proud and beautiful; an Eastern city of wonder whose brothers the mountains are. It was not like any city of Earth, for above purple mists rose towers, spires, and pyramids which one may only dream of in opiate lands beyond the Oxus . . . Only Dunsany could fashion its equal, and he in dreams only." He would later come to hate New York and everything he felt it represented.

One night, Sonia threw a dinner party for Lovecraft,

Loveman, a writer and mutual friend named Frank Belknap Long, and Sonia's grown daughter, Florence. Lovecraft deemed Florence Greene, who was about twenty years old, a "flapper." He found her to be a "pert, spoiled, and ultra-independent infant rather more hard-boiled of visage than her benignant mater." Sonia could be tough, he figured, but her daughter was tougher.

Lovecraft, who had lived rather frugally, was continually amazed at the sheer quantity of food devoured by Sonia, their mutual friends, and indeed all New Yorkers. The feast Sonia bought for her guests at a midtown Italian restaurant on another occasion particularly astonished him. The meal was capped by an outing to the theater to see a musical, which Lovecraft enjoyed. Afterward, Sonia bought everyone dessert, this time at a Russian eatery.

Later in the week, Lovecraft went up to 100th Street and West End Avenue to the home of Frank Belknap Long and his family—"an exquisite boy of twenty who hardly looks fifteen," as he described him—and his parents. Lovecraft was delighted by the Long's two parrots and their cat named Felis. Frank Belknap Long had written a piece for Lovecraft's *Conservative* that was inspired by the cat. Joined by Loveman, they then went on a trip to the Edgar Allan Poe cottage in the Fordham section of the city. Finding it closed, they had to return the next day.

Lovecraft found the Poe cottage to be "a small world of magic." He was mesmerized by the chair and desk where Poe wrote "Annabel Lee," and the very bed where

A visit to the cottage where Edgar Allan Poe wrote many of his tales thrilled Lovecraft. *(Courtesy of the Library of Congress.)*

Poe's young wife breathed her last. He identified with Poe's struggles against poverty and his fervid desire to be an artist. He was overwhelmed at the thought of being in the same place where his idol, his master as he called him, had lived, breathed, and worked on so many masterpieces. He found it very hard to simply walk away from the cottage and everything it stood for.

Lovecraft also went sightseeing with a long-time friend and fellow amateur journalist named Rheinhart Kleiner, whom he always referred to as "Klei." They walked down Fifth Avenue to Washington Square in Greenwich Village, and on another occasion visited lower Manhattan. Lovecraft found Chinatown to be clean and pleasant, but was appalled by what he thought of as the squalor and filthiness of the slums of the Lower East Side. "A bastard mess of stewing mongrel flesh without intellect, repellent to eye, nose and imagination," is how he described it.

As usual, Lovecraft could not relate to and was revolted by "foreigners" and any people who were different from him. To his mind, they were not refined and genteel.

It was with mixed emotions that Lovecraft finally departed New York City. He slept all the way home on the train. Back in Providence, he had many wonderful memories stored up, but he was also glad to be home. He was, however, not averse to traveling again, this time to visit Samuel Loveman (who had also left New York) and another friend, the composer Alfred Galpin, in Cleveland, Ohio. Lovecraft left for Cleveland in August, four months after his trip to New York. He found the Ohio scenery from the train windows vastly inferior to the fields and forests of New England. Lovecraft and Galpin had corresponded but never met. At the train station in Cleveland, they recognized each other from snapshots they had exchanged.

Although Lovecraft was only thirty-two, he constantly referred to himself as "grandpa" or the "old gentleman." This was in part because many of his acquaintances were much younger than he was. These he would call "kid" or "grandson." It was also because Lovecraft felt as if he were out of his own time, someone who had been born 150 years too late. His obsession with customs and styles of a bygone era often made him feel antiquated.

In Cleveland, Lovecraft stayed with his "grandson" Alfred Galpin, who proved almost as generous a host as Sonia Greene. The two would go around the corner to Samuel Loveman's apartment to have cultural discussions. Lovecraft was impressed with their knowledge of the arts and hoped to learn more from them about music and painting. Galpin introduced Lovecraft to the music of Chopin. They toured the city in automobiles, and met with a rare book dealer named George Kirk, who also owned a bookshop in the Chelsea section of Manhattan. Lovecraft was introduced to the great poet Hart Crane, whose work he came to admire. Kirk and Crane became part of Lovecraft's ever widening circle of friends and correspondents.

It was so hot in Cleveland, and his main companion Alfred Galpin was so much younger than he, that Lovecraft relaxed some of his standards while in Ohio. He wore his hat only on formal occasions and exchanged his vest for a belt with his initial on the buckle. He wrote to his friends that they would not believe the change that had come over him. He reported he had not felt so cheerful in years. "What I need," he wrote, "is the constant company of youthful and congenial literary persons." He was also happy because a problem he had been experiencing with ingrown facial hairs and the blemishes they caused had cleared up to a great extent while he was in Cleveland.

Lovecraft was able to stay in Cleveland longer than expected because Alfred Galpin paid for most of his meals and entertainment. What Galpin did not pay for, Samuel Loveman or George Kirk usually did. Lovecraft was becoming accustomed to accepting the generosity of others.

In September of that same year, Lovecraft returned

to New York City for another short visit. As usual, Sonia put him up and fed him, and he explored sections of the city he had missed on his first trip. On this occasion, he learned an ancient church that had been part of the old Dutch village now known as Flatbush was still standing. Lovecraft investigated this place early one evening, and as expected, it excited his imagination. "As I viewed this village churchyard in the autumn twilight, the city seemed to fade from sight, and give place to the Netherland town of long ago." He chipped off a piece of a crumbling 1747 gravestone and imagined some *thing* pulling out of the graveyard dirt to come after him for desecrating his tomb. This became the basis of his story "The Hound" (1922).

Only two months later, Lovecraft was on the move

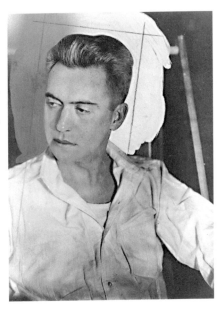

Lovecraft admired the poetry of Hart Crane, and the two became friends. *(Courtesy of the Library of Congress.)*

Lovecraft enjoyed the atmosphere of Marblehead, Massachusetts, and used his impressions of the town in "The Festival." *(Courtesy of the Library of Congress.)*

again, heading for Salem, Massachusetts, site of the infamous witch trials. From there he went to the nearby fishing port of Marblehead, which had a tremendous effect on him. He was amazed that the town seemed little changed since 1770, when it was most prosperous. It seemed like a place he had visited—which could only be visited—in his dreams. "General Washington could tomorrow ride horseback down the street named for him without the least sensation of strangeness," he wrote. He felt it was the living embodiment of the eighteenth century, as much an anachronism as Lovecraft was. Lovecraft used his impressions of Marblehead in his 1923 story "The Festival."

By this time, Lovecraft had written about twenty-five short stories, very few of which had been published. Those he had published in *Home Brew*, *Herbert West: Reanimator* and *The Lurking Fear*, he considered to be substandard. On the horizon was a new, more prestigious venue for his work, which would provide him nearly regular publication.

Chapter Four

Parkside Avenue

In 1923, Lovecraft was thirty-three years of age. He had few commercially published works. He was not paid for the articles and letters printed in the assorted amateur journals he either contributed to or edited himself. He found the work published in the magazine that did pay him, *Home Brew,* to be beneath his usual standards. The major magazines, the so-called slicks like *Smart Set* or *Saturday Evening Post,* did not appreciate his style and did not publish stories in the fantasy-horror genre. The Jazz Age was just beginning, and the higher paying magazines were publishing stories by F. Scott Fitzgerald, Ernest Hemingway, and other young authors who wrote about their college and war experiences in a crisp, economical style. Lovecraft's work was about as far from this type of fiction as possible.

The increase in literacy, and the development of a new type of magazine, was about to provide an outlet for Lovecraft's fiction, as well as that of dozens of other

popular writers. In the 1920s, a number of "pulp" magazines began to appear on the newsstands. These were
digest-sized periodicals that were printed on the very
cheapest paper—made from pulpwood—hence their
name. Pulp magazines generally published popular fiction churned out by "hack" writers who were paid by
the word and wrote prodigiously. In the days before
comic books, there were pulp magazines devoted to the
exploits of "super" characters such as The Shadow and
Doc Savage, forerunners of the comic book characters
Batman and Superman. There were also science fiction,
mystery and detective, adventure, love story, and West-
ern pulps. The one that came to Lovecraft's rescue,
Weird Tales, was devoted to horror and dark fantasy
fiction.

The first issue of *Weird Tales* hit newsstands in March
1923. The magazine struggled to gain popularity. Publishers Jacob Clark Henneberger and J.M. Lassinger
hired Edwin Baird, a mystery writer and former news-
paper man, as editor. Baird was not a "natural" in editing supernatural fiction, but he held the publication
together long enough to establish its initial readership
and cultivate relationships with the first authors. *Weird
Tales* also employed Farnsworth Wright as its "first
reader"—an employee who read manuscripts and decided if they were worth consideration for publication.
Wright later became editor and led the magazine into
its period of greatest quality and profitability during
the 1930s. He had a sharp instinct for macabre fiction
and published writers such as Tennessee Williams, Otis

Adelbert Kline, Robert E. Howard, Seabury Quinn, and of course, Lovecraft.

Lovecraft did not make it easy for Baird to buy his stories. He mailed five pieces at one time with a cover letter—a stunt almost guaranteed to raise the hackles of any editor. First, he mentioned how many times the stories had been rejected. Next, he assured Baird he was in no way a writer who cared about popular tastes, which could not have pleased an editor who was hoping to attract new readers. Next, he insisted the stories be published without a single change, not even reasonable copyediting. Finally, he ended with a critique of the stories he had read in an earlier issue of *Weird Tales*, damning most as enjoyable but conventional. The letter was written in Lovecraft's most condescending tone. It seems he was so sure he would be rejected by this inferior pulp that he was practically doing his best to ensure it, so that his ego would not be as badly bruised.

Another editor might have tossed Lovecraft's stories in the trash bin, but Baird was curious enough to give them a read. He read between the lines of the insolent cover letter and knew, far from being indifferent, Lovecraft was very anxious to be published in *Weird Tales*. Ironically, the cover letter made it clear the man could write. Baird needed a steady supply of good horror fiction, and after reading the stories, recognized Lovecraft's work was far superior to most being submitted to *Weird Tales*.

Of the five stories Lovecraft sent to Baird, he chose "Dagon" (1917) and "The Statement of Randolph

Carter" (1919) for publication. Over the years, Baird and subsequent editors of *Weird Tales* would buy many short stories from Lovecraft. Some of these, such as "Arthur Jermyn," a.k.a. "The White Ape" (1920) had been written years earlier, others were brand new and written specifically for *Weird Tales*. These included one of Lovecraft's horror masterpieces, "The Rats in the Walls" (1923).

Lovecraft originally submitted "The Rats in the Walls" to *Argosy All-Story Weekly* (the two publications merged in 1920). That periodical's editor found it, as Lovecraft put it, "too horrible for the tender sensibilities of a delicately nurtured publick [sic]." Although "The Rats in the Walls" is now generally considered one of Lovecraft's best stories, he disparaged it in later years. "My criticism of the tale is not the same as yours," he wrote one fan that thought it took too long to get going. "I approve of leisurely development. To me the climax now seems crudely and sensationally handled—my typical 1923 stuff." Lovecraft got the idea for the story from the sound of crinkling wallpaper. A man, searching for the title creatures, descends into massive catacombs beneath his ancient home only to learn a shocking secret about his family's past.

In another cover letter to Baird, Lovecraft spelled out his own theories of great horror fiction. The letter had a tone as though he were instructing the editor—which, of course, he was. "Only a cynic can create horror," he told Baird. "For behind every masterpiece of the sort must reside a driving daemonic [sic] force

Lovecraft ghost-wrote a story for escape artist Harry Houdini that appeared in *Weird Tales*. *(Courtesy of the Library of Congress.)*

that despises the human race and its illusions, and longs to pull them to pieces and mock them."

Most of Lovecraft's work was so well-received at *Weird Tales* that owner J.C. Henneberger chose Lovecraft to ghostwrite a story for the famous magician Harry Houdini. Henneberger thought it would be a real coup to have a story by Houdini in its pages. Baird recommended Lovecraft as a fast, prolific worker. Of course, both Baird and Henneberger also knew Lovecraft could use the money. They figured correctly that Lovecraft would not be above doing something "commercial" if he could control the quality of the piece, and the price was right.

Henneberger gave Lovecraft the outline of the plot, as related to him by Houdini. It took place in Cairo,

Egypt, around the Sphinx and under the Great Pyramid, and was supposedly factual. It turned out Houdini had made the whole thing up, but Lovecraft proceeded with the commission anyway. Since he wrote the story in the first person, as if Houdini himself were narrating, he received no byline. The story was published as "Imprisoned with the Pharaohs," a.k.a. "Under the Pyramids" (1924).

On March 3, 1924, Lovecraft and Sonia Greene were wed. It is not known which of them first had the idea of matrimony, but it is known that Sonia's daughter was not overjoyed at the union.

It is likely the two decided to wed more for simple companionship than out of any deep love or mutual attraction. Lovecraft saw Sonia as a kind of patroness. With her income as a base, he could afford to write what he wanted and eschew commercial factors. He admitted to his Aunt Lillian that the financial aspect was an important factor.

He had also come to rely upon Sonia's steady encouragement and intellectual stimulus as much as her money. Concerning Sonia, as Lovecraft saw it, he "would come not as a burden but as the filler of a lonely void and the bearer of aesthetic and intellectual congeniality to one who had not found this quality in others."

Lovecraft also reasoned that if he shared her apartment on Parkside Avenue, Sonia would have to pay no more rent than she was already paying. He assured his aunt that he would contribute to the "common fund" as much as he was able. He intimated that the marriage was an alternative to destitution, loneliness, and eventual suicide. As he often did, Lovecraft reiterated the facts, as he saw them, of his "delicate" and "sensitive" nature. Throughout his life, Lovecraft would use this excuse to explain away many of his more peculiar actions.

The day before the wedding, Lovecraft arrived in New York, where Sonia was waiting for him. She took him to see a friend named Miss Tucker, who ran a bookstore and had many literary connections. Sonia wanted to have Miss Tucker's opinion as to the likelihood of Lovecraft finding employment in the publishing field. Miss Tucker told them Lovecraft was a tal-

Sonia's Brooklyn apartment was just a few blocks from Prospect Park.
(Courtesy of the Library of Congress.)

ented writer and thought she could help him find placement. The morning of the wedding, Tucker and Lovecraft met again, where she tested him on proofreading and copy-editing.

After lunch, he and Sonia took out a marriage license at the Brooklyn borough hall. Using her own money, Sonia bought a platinum ring with diamond chips for eighty-five dollars. Lovecraft promised to repay her for the ring when he could afford to do so. Afterward, the two were married in the historic St. Paul's Chapel on Broadway and Vesey Street in Manhattan. Lovecraft loved the antiquity of the chapel, built in 1766, but later referred to it as the *"Place de la Guillotine."* This certainly indicates a level of mixed emotions about his marriage.

Lovecraft and his new bride honeymooned in Philadelphia. They spent most of their wedding night at a public stenographer's office, where they rented a typewriter for a dollar. Lovecraft had been in such a hurry to catch the train to New York that he left the typescript of "Imprisoned with the Pharaohs" in the Providence train station. Luckily, he still had his original handwritten copy. Sonia dictated from this copy while Lovecraft typed. He was delighted that Sonia could read his "careless scrawl" and figured she could be a big help in copying his manuscripts in the future. They toured Philadelphia the following day, and in the evening did more typing. "Truly a most practical and industrious honeymoon," Lovecraft described it.

With his wife paying the rent and food bills, Lovecraft

enjoyed the first couple of months as a husband. Freed from responsibility, he should have been able to write at a frantic clip. However, he found himself distracted by friends and the attractions of the city. The marriage grew even tenser when Sonia developed financial problems. She had sunk most of her capital into a hat shop venture that went bankrupt. Only four months into the marriage, she had to tell Lovecraft she could no longer support the two of them. As Lovecraft's income from writing and editing was minuscule at best, he would have to find a job.

The marriage may have been doomed to failure because of Lovecraft's psychological state. "The invalidism and seclusion of my earlier years had left me, at thirty-three, as naive and inexperienced and unused to dealings with the world as most are at seventeen or eighteen," he wrote in a biographical sketch many years later.

> I had only just burst out of a shell of retirement, and was finding the external world as novel and fascinating as a kid finds it . . . my whole psychology was that of a belated adolescent, with the usual egotism, pompous writing, jauntiness, and show-off tendencies of the callow . . . I thought I was quite a guy. I had a better time then than I have now, but only because I didn't realise [sic] what a vacuous, snobbish, and complacent ass I was.

Even with Miss Tucker making inquiries for him,

Lovecraft could not find employment in the publishing field. In late July, Lovecraft answered an ad placed by the Creditors' National Clearing House in Newark, New Jersey. He learned the firm was seeking young men to promote their debt-collecting services to other businesses. Given a packet of material to study, he revised the suggested sales speech overnight. The firm immediately adopted it.

It was possible he could have had a bright future with Creditors' National, were it not for one major obstacle. His first day on the job, as he canvassed for clients, he realized he did not have the qualities to make a good salesman. "I lack the magnetism, or brass, or whatever wizardry" it required, he felt. Lovecraft thought an effective salesman had to be pushy, but he found pushiness to be boorish and vulgar. He simply could not bring himself to do it. He decided he had to find work as a writer or editor. Nothing else would suit him.

In the meantime, Sonia found employment at a hat shop. The owner asked Sonia to provide the names and addresses of the customers of her own failed millinery business. Sonia agreed, but as soon as she did, she was let go. The only steady income Lovecraft could count on was the rent on some family property back in Rhode Island. It averaged around six dollars per month.

In desperation, he placed the following ad in the *New York Times*:

WRITER AND REVISER, free-lance, desires regular and permanent salaried connection with any responsible enterprise requiring literary services; exceptionally thorough experience in preparing correct and fluent text on subjects assigned, and in meeting the most difficult, intricate and extensive problems of rewriting and constructive revision, prose or verse; would also consider situation dealing with such proofreading as demands rapidness and a keenly developed sense of the niceties of English usage; age 34, married.

In addition to placing the ad, Lovecraft circulated a very erudite letter explaining he had to resort to unusual methods to obtain a job because of his complete lack of experience in virtually any field aside from writing. (Not to mention the lack of a college degree.) He told prospective employers he was recently married and therefore desired a steadier income than that afforded a freelance writer.

Neither his ad nor his letter attracted any offers of employment of the type he desired. It was clear a man of uncommon intelligence and education drafted them, but their verbosity and somewhat defensive tone may have been off-putting to many prospective employers. His aggressive cultivation probably intimidated some recipients of the letter. In any case, his lack of job experience was a hurdle he could not overcome. He would walk from door to door, only to experience one rejection after another, "a weary and detestable tramp," as he termed it.

On August 21, 1924, Lovecraft took a long walking

tour during the late night hours with his friend George Kirk. The two men explored what Lovecraft referred to as the "colonial part" of New York City. Lovecraft was particularly interested in the different architectural styles of the surrounding buildings. He noted the brick townhouses in Abingdon Square in Greenwich Village, the "utter and poignant charm" of Patchin Place and other Village byways, and the winding streets that led to Minetta Lane.

"All the Italian squalor was faded into shadow," he wrote, "and I could fancy spotless periwigs and sedan chairs under the wan, waning half moon that struggled above the lines of antique gables." From Greenwich Village, Lovecraft and his companion walked down Varick Street, then east past Broadway, and down onto Pearl Street in the financial section of the city. "By the time we reached City Hall it was morning."

Sonia, however, could not get to sleep until her husband came home. This meant Lovecraft either had to forgo his nightly jaunts with friends, or stay out with the constant tension of knowing his wife was anxiously waiting up for him. He began to refer to her as the "ball and chain." He told friends he longed for the days when he had only been Sonia's guest and could come and go as he pleased. "She never knew when I came back—or if I came back at all."

Lovecraft may not have worked and did very little writing, but he nonetheless kept busy. It was around this time he received a letter from his friend W. Paul Cook, who was starting a fan magazine devoted to the horror field. He asked Lovecraft to contribute an authoritative essay exploring the history of horror literature, with a focus on Poe, Machen, and even earlier writers. Despite the fact that there was to be no payment for the piece, Lovecraft took the assignment seriously. Reading was certainly no chore for him. Even when he began writing again, he was able to squeeze in the perusal of dozens of books and stories by earlier authors between the time it took to compose his own pieces.

It took him three years to do what he felt was proper justice to the historical survey requested by Cook. In 1927, it was finally published in *The Recluse,* the only issue of the amateur magazine to ever appear. (It has become a collector's item worth several hundred dollars.) Even after initial publication, Lovecraft kept adding to and fine-tuning the essay. It was serialized in another amateur publication called *The Fantasy Fan* in the early thirties. After Lovecraft's death, a small publisher in New York, Ben Abramson, published the long piece in book form as *Supernatural Horror in Literature*.

In his essay, Lovecraft wrote:

> The appeal of the spectrally macabre is generally narrow because it demands from the reader a certain degree of imagination and a capacity for detachment from everyday life ... but the sensitive are always with us ... no amount of rationalisation [sic], reform, or Freudian analysis can quite annul the thrill of the

chimney-corner whisper or the lonely wood. We must judge a weird tale not by the author's intent, or by the mere mechanics of the plot; but by the emotional level which it attains at its least mundane point. If the proper sensations are excited, such a 'high spot' must be admitted on its own merits as weird literature, no matter how prosaically it is later dragged down. The one test of the really weird is simply this—whether or not there be excited in the reader a profound sense of dread, and of contact with unknown spheres and powers; a subtle attitude of awed listening, as if for the beating of black wings or the scratching of outside shapes and entities on the known universe's utmost rim. And of course, the more completely and unifiedly a story conveys this atmosphere, the better it is as a work of art in the given medium.

Lovecraft had plenty of theories, but his writing "career" had come to a standstill. His marriage had turned from a thing of convenience to an exhausting series of arguments and recriminations, usually about money. He saw his friends and explored the city, but wrote no stories. Neither he nor his wife could find work. Only married a few months, Mr. and Mrs. Lovecraft sank ever more deeply into a miasma of disillusionment, health problems, and poverty.

Chapter Five

The Horrors of Red Hook

Not long after their wedding, before she lost her money in the hat shop, Sonia put a down payment on a property in Bryn Mawr Park in Yonkers. The plan had been to build a house on the property at some later point. Before long, the installments on the property were overdue. Not only were Sonia and Lovecraft not fated to live together in a new house, they were to spend much of the rest of their married life in separate dwellings in separate cities.

Due to the combination of marital and financial troubles, Sonia's nerves were so strained that she had to be hospitalized. Although one doctor recommended gall bladder surgery, Sonia's gastric disorders were probably caused by stress. While Sonia recuperated in Brooklyn Hospital, Lovecraft experimented with making his own meals and keeping the apartment clean. When Sonia was released from the hospital in late October 1924, she and Lovecraft briefly stayed at a farmhouse in South Somerville, New Jersey. Lovecraft traveled back to Philadelphia, where they had honeymooned, while his wife convalesced. It is likely the money for the "rest cure" came from his Aunt Lillian.

In December 1924, Sonia felt well enough to accept an offer of employment from a large department store in Cincinnati, Ohio. The job meant she had to live in Cincinnati, returning to New York for a week every few months. The Lovecrafts gave up the large apartment on Parkside Avenue and looked for more modest quarters for him to stay in. With the assistance of his Aunt Lillian, Lovecraft found an apartment at 169 Clinton Street in Brooklyn Heights. This was a boarding house right at the edge of the Red Hook section of Brooklyn.

While Sonia was working in Ohio, Lovecraft hung out with his friends and continued to tour the historic sections of the city. Lovecraft referred to himself and these friends as The Kalem Club, because all of their last names began with the letters "K," "L," or "M." An exception—and nominal member of the club—was the poet Hart Crane. Crane's fiendish bouts of drinking greatly alarmed the always-sober Lovecraft. Lovecraft persuaded George Kirk to take the room above him in the boarding house, but Kirk moved into Manhattan after a few months.

Eventually, Lovecraft realized he was spending too much time with the Kalem Club and not enough time writing. The depression he felt over the state of his finances and marriage undoubtedly made it difficult for him to write. However, he finally woke up to the fact

Lovecraft's stay at this boarding house on Clinton Street served as inspiration for "The Horror at Red Hook." *(Courtesy of Brown University.)*

that he had to get to work if their financial state were to improve. When George Kirk or Samuel Loveman dropped by his room, as they had gotten in the habit of doing, he politely, but firmly, asked them to leave. He got into fewer long conversations and went on fewer walking tours of the city. Even with this new resolve, he only completed one or two stories during this period.

At first, Lovecraft liked living in the boarding house. The minute he heard the English accent of the landlady, Mrs. Burns, he was won over. He at first thought she was refined, and her two sons cultivated. "Only later was I to learn of her shrewish tongue, desperate household negligence, miserly watchfulness of lights and unwatchfulness of repairs, and reckless indifference to the class of lodger she admitted," he complained.

Lovecraft claimed Mrs. Burns did not bother with references. It had become clear to him that she could get few tenants of the "quality" she originally desired and now was only after the money. He told friends that he rarely saw the other denizens of the boarding house, only heard them and the strange sounds they made. Lovecraft, prejudiced and snobbish, could not deal with the fact that many of his fellow boarders were "Turks" and "Syrians." In his letters during the period, Lovecraft makes these foreign boarders sound every bit as malevolent as the "old ones" in his horror stories. In fact, while living at 169 Clinton, he wrote "The Horror at Red Hook."

"The Horror at Red Hook" (1925) deals with a cult of devil worshipers who kidnap children, make human sacrifices, and do all manner of evil in the hidden rooms and tunnels below the town of Red Hook. It is more than intimated that these miscreants are worse than mere evil-doers and kidnappers—they are also worshippers of alien, horrible entities that are just waiting to spread their malevolence throughout all the Earth. Lovecraft so hated and feared the immigrants who inhabited the neighborhood that he could almost imagine them actually doing the hideous things he ascribed to them in his story. While "The Horror at Red Hook" is full of almost comical overstatement about the Brooklyn neighborhood and its denizens, it also displays Lovecraft's brilliant descriptive prowess and ability to chill. Like many of his works, it is as frightening for what it does not say as for what it does.

Lovecraft simply could not relate to the many foreigners he saw in New York. Even native-born New Yorkers seemed alien to him, moving at a much faster pace than citizens of Providence. The man who had spent so many years hiding from the world in his peaceful room found it difficult to deal with so many people at once. The fact that they spoke in strange tongues, wore unusual clothing, and had differing goals and values only made it worse.

Lovecraft thought his erudition and aristocratic deportment made him superior to other men of his own race. He found it hard to even think of men of other races—Jews, blacks, immigrants—as being entirely human. Lovecraft was not alone in his thinking, unfortunately, but other men who felt as he did usually softened their views as they got to know people from other races. Lovecraft, who maintained his rigid views and refused to get to know his neighbors, became even more racist in his opinions while living in New York. The crowded streets and multi-ethnic population only tended to validate, in his own mind, the bigotry he had developed on a more intellectual level growing up in Providence. He perceived the mostly uneducated, poorly-dressed foreigners around him as pigs in a filthy sty.

In spite of the fact his wife was Jewish, he remained fiercely anti-Semitic. "The mass of contemporary Jews are hopeless as far as America is concerned. They are the product of alien blood, and inherit alien ideals . . . I've easily felt able to slaughter a score or two when jammed in a N.Y. subway train," he wrote. "Superior semites"—of which we can assume he numbered his wife—"can be assimilated *one by one* by the dominant

Aryan when they sever all ties of association and memory with the mass of organized Jewry."

It was not uncommon to find other Americans with these anti-Semitic opinions during the pre-World War II period. There were even many who supported Adolph Hitler in Germany before the onset of the war. Lovecraft supported some of Hitler's theories, but he also termed Hitler an "unscientific extremist" whose racial assumptions were "crude and ignorant." When a young Jewish fan named Kenneth Sterling showed up in Providence to visit Lovecraft, he was impressed with Sterling's intelligence and precociousness. "I wouldn't for the world discourage him in his endeavors. He really does seem . . . astonishingly promising." Lovecraft's late story "In the Walls of Eryx" (1935) was written from a premise that came from Sterling, who later became a respected physician.

On an outing to Pelham Bay Park in the Bronx, Lovecraft was disconcerted to discover more black people than white. He was also condescending towards Asians, Latinos, Italians, the Irish, French-Canadians, and others. He cared little for any ethnic group outside of Aryans and Anglo-Saxons. However, while he certainly had racist attitudes, his talk of murder and genocide has to be taken with a grain of salt. As his protégé Robert Bloch put it, "If Lovecraft was a racist we must recognize that the term was not generally considered pejorative during his own time. In the twenties and thirties, Anglo-Saxon superiority was virtually taken for granted not only in literature but in daily life."

Lovecraft's racial views were also caused by the obvious inferiority complex that lurked beneath his air of superiority. He proclaimed himself better than other men, but he was barely making a dime. He mostly lived off the earnings of his wife and aunts, and was homely and odd. He had a delicate nervous disposition that kept him from having a career. He consoled himself with the thought that he was superior to, not only the foreign-speaking rabble that "infested" the streets of New York like cockroaches, but to just about everyone else. He began to see this rabble—and his lack of success—as being inseparable from the city. He preferred to go out late at night, instead of during the daytime, so that he would encounter as few people as possible.

In early 1925, Lovecraft was hopeful he could finally support himself through his writing, albeit, a different type of writing from horror fiction. He briefly entertained the notion of becoming a freelance copywriter. He would be able to work in his apartment and write advertisements that might, or might not, be bought by the companies whose services he extolled. Although Lovecraft insisted he was too experienced to get overly excited about his prospects, his letters reveal that he was counting very heavily on the copy writing working out. "I can see myself . . . with an actual income and possible future for the first time in my life," he wrote. Although he did put together a few ads, the venture did not pan out.

Things were not working out well for Sonia, either. The long separations from her husband, and the commutes from the Midwest to New York and back again were not good for her nerves. Twice she had to be admitted to a private hospital in Cincinnati. Finally, she had to quit her job, which she found much too stressful. It was decided she should take another rest cure as she had the previous year. This time, Lovecraft remained at home while Sonia stayed with a female doctor in Saratoga Springs.

During this period, Lovecraft found it easy to get rid of the weight he had gained while living with Sonia. She had fed him well and often, but could no longer afford to do so. Lovecraft talked of his "dieting," but it was more a diet of necessity than choice. Making economical decisions at the supermarket, he would live for days on sandwiches of bread, beans, and Swiss cheese. He would hunt all over Brooklyn for the stores that sold these and other items at the lowest prices.

In May 1925, Lovecraft's attitude toward Red Hook in particular and New York City in general took another nosedive. During one evening while he slept, his room was robbed of many of his and Sonia's possessions. Some radio parts that Lovecraft had been storing for Samuel Loveman were also stolen. Lovecraft was particularly upset that the thieves had not left him with a single good suit. He suspected some young men who lived next door were the culprits. By the time a detective came to talk to Lovecraft, these youths had disappeared. Lovecraft partly blamed himself for not securely bolting a connecting door between his apartment and the next. He was gratified the villains at least had not taken any of his precious books or mementos.

Lovecraft set out to find replacements for the clothing that was taken. He was particularly obsessed with finding one good suit for special occasions. "A gentleman should be always attired in good taste, but he should never be actively conscious of his clothes," he wrote. "They should be to him integral outgrowths of his personality and aesthetick [sic] sense." Going from one cheap store on 14th Street in Manhattan to another, he came across a crumpled suit that nevertheless had the cut and feel he desired. Lovecraft was ecstatic when he learned the suit cost only $11.95—and came with an extra pair of trousers.

When Sonia returned to New York from Saratoga Springs, the couple had to face their usual problems. Lovecraft's aunts wondered if it might not be better for him to return to Providence—without Sonia. A feeling of gratitude and responsibility toward his wife at first prevented Lovecraft from seriously considering this option. Desperate for cash, he went to work for his friend Samuel Loveman's bookstore in early 1926. His job was simply to address envelopes in which ten thousand catalogues would be mailed to potential clients. Lovecraft was paid $17.50 a week for this tedious but hardly taxing labor.

During the brief time he was married and lived in New York, he traveled outside the city as often as possible. On trips to Washington, D.C., and Virginia, he found the people "less repulsive and Mongrel." He was always trying to find an oasis that reminded him of the more placid Providence. He found it in Elizabeth, New Jersey, where he felt sufficiently at peace to actually get some writing done. Elizabeth also provided Lovecraft with inspiration. A creepy old house on Bridge Street and Elizabeth Avenue prompted him to write his great "ghost" story "The Shunned House" (1924). It was in Scott Park in Elizabeth that Lovecraft sat down one sunny afternoon and penned the dark, gothic "He" (1925) with its undertones of Poe's "Fall of the House of Usher."

"He" is the tale of an unhappy man, the narrator, who is clearly Lovecraft. In Greenwich Village, he meets up with a soul mate who responds to his longing for the better days of past centuries. This old man takes him through torturous alleyways to a crumbling manse, which offers views of previous decades from its windows. After the narrator sees a view of the horrible future he is afraid awaits the world, he cries out—and brings a terrible doom down upon the head of his host. The house literally crumbles into its foundation.

The opening lines of "He" make clear Lovecraft's mental state at the time of their composition:

> My coming to New York had been a mistake; for whereas I had looked for poignant wonder and inspiration in the teeming labyrinths of ancient streets ... and in the Cyclopean modern towers and pinnacles that rise blackly Babylonian under waning moons, I had found instead only a sense of horror and oppression which threatened to master, paralyze, and annihilate me.

Chapter Six

Creative Peak

Lovecraft wanted to return to Providence. Sonia knew this, but he hesitated to leave her. Sonia understood her husband as few people did. She put up with his moods, continually encouraged him, made him feel wanted and welcome, and comforted him over his setbacks.

"Each financial shortcoming of mine is accepted and condoned as soon as it is proved inevitable," he wrote about his wife. He found akin to saintliness her "devotion which can accept this combination of incompetence and aesthetic selfishness without a murmur." Yet Lovecraft felt no true passion, or even abiding love, for Sonia. His primary emotions toward her were gratitude and guilt over his shameless use of her. Nevertheless, he always claimed Sonia had his respect and admiration, and he felt genuine affection for her.

When Sonia was offered a new job opportunity in Ohio, this time in Cleveland at the Halle department store, Lovecraft stayed on in New York. His aunts suggested he should relocate to Boston or Cambridge, where they thought there were better literary opportunities. Knowing how sick her husband was of New York, Sonia told him she would also seek employment in Boston.

Nothing came of their talk of moving to Boston together. Sonia might have taken too long to return from Ohio, or Lovecraft was too determined to return to Providence, but they were incapable of deciding on future plans that would keep them together. Sonia would have made sacrifices to keep her marriage intact, but Lovecraft was more interested in returning to Rhode Island. He saw no real future for himself and Sonia. She had once had money, but now both were struggling for every dollar. From his perspective, if they were going to have to endure poverty, he would rather do it in Providence. The financial problems cut both ways. Despite Sonia's usual positive attitude, she sometimes got impatient with Lovecraft's constant poverty and dependency. This became the topic of most of their arguments. After two years of marriage, he left Brooklyn— and Sonia—in late March of 1926.

Years later, Lovecraft claimed the thought of moving to a "backwater" like Providence while undergoing financial chaos was too much for his wife. She "found such a prospect . . . nothing short of asphyxiation!" He implied it was Sonia's decision to stay in New York and not follow him. It is doubtful, however, she was ever given the option of moving to Providence with her husband. More likely, Lovecraft saw the move as a second chance for the bachelor life he had coveted since 1924. Essentially, Lovecraft abandoned Sonia.

"I haven't a doubt but that matrimony can become a very helpful and pleasing permanent arrangement when both parties happen to harbour the potentialities of parallel mental and imaginative lives," Lovecraft wrote some years later. "But I must add that I don't see how the hell any couple outside of professional psychiatrists can ever tell whether or not they possess this genuine parallelism until the actual test of two or three years of joint family life." Lovecraft also mused celibacy was a small price to pay for independence.

For the rest of his life, Lovecraft was unable to be objective about New York City. He had not been successful there, which meant it was a place of unlimited "horrors." Essentially a small-town soul, Lovecraft simply could not deal with the energy, enormity, and anonymity of such a big city. "New York is dead," he wrote, "and the brilliancy which so impresses one from outside is the phosphorescence of a maggoty corpse." There were no true artists, no culture, in New York, he ranted, only posers; it was simply a vast wasteland. "The 'aesthetes' of New York are less interested in art and beauty than in themselves," he said.

Lovecraft, however, never really sought out the many cultivated people who lived in and around New York. In reality, the 1920s were in many ways a golden age in the city. Most of the nation's best writers either lived or spent long stretches of time there. It was the era of the Harlem Renaissance and jazz was emerging as a major art form. The theaters on and off Broadway staged plays by Eugene O'Neill and George Bernard Shaw and others. There were countless ways to participate in the cultural life of New York, and by extension, the entire nation. Lovecraft, however, confined himself almost exclusively to out-of-town friends whom he found less intimidating. He did not attend concerts, the ballet, or the opera, and rarely went to the theater.

Obsessed with his own failures, he was unwilling to see any value in New York or its inhabitants. Lovecraft assumed his own experiences were the norm and was incapable of seeing the world from any but his own perspective. "Not even the threat of damnation could induce me to dwell in the accursed place again," he wrote. However, Lovecraft did admit there had been things he liked about the city: "The skyline, the sunsets over Central Park . . . It may be that younger, gayer souls than I can find something endurable in Manhattan. They are welcome to it."

Lovecraft was ecstatic to be back in Providence in 1926. "Providence is part of me," he wrote. As usual, he depended on the kindness of loved ones when he returned. His Aunt Lillian let him share her small apartment at 10 Barnes Street in an old Colonial neighborhood. The 1880 house had been converted into apartments. His ground-floor room was originally a dining room and had a fireplace. He referred to his aunt's domestic servant, Delilah, as "the faithful negress."

Not far from Barnes Street was the infamous Halsey Mansion, which was said to be haunted. Lovecraft made it the setting for his novel *The Case of Charles Dexter*

Upon his return to Providence, Lovecraft shared his Aunt Lillian's small apartment at 10 Barnes Street. *(Courtesy of Brown University.)*

Ward (1927-1928), which he wrote the following year. In fact, in the six months following his return to Rhode Island, he wrote copiously. He produced several stories and four short novels.

The title character of *The Case of Charles Dexter Ward* is the descendant of Joseph Curwen. Years before, Curwen had been killed by the townspeople after performing unholy experiments. (Lovecraft named Captain Whipple, the leader of the band of men who destroy Curwen, after his beloved grandfather.) Ward himself seems possessed by his ancestor and continues Curwen's research. Curwen had wanted to resuscitate the bodies of long-dead geniuses to acquire their knowledge. It turns out that Ward has brought his ancestor back to life, and Curwen eventually takes his descendant's place. While as atmospheric and interesting as most of Lovecraft's work, *The Case of Charles Dexter Ward* is not as effective as his short stories.

The more intriguing novella *The Dream Quest Of*

Unknown Kadath (1926-1927) is a suspenseful and often harrowing work in which Randolph Carter is intrigued and bedeviled by glimpses of a magnificent golden city he sees in his dreams. (Carter, an alter-ego for Lovecraft, had already appeared in a number of short stories, most of which were inspired by Lovecraft's dreams.) While asleep, however, he never gets past the high terrace surrounding the city. He is so fascinated by what he sees that he becomes desperate to enter and reside forever in this glittering domain. He decides to try to find Kadath, the home of the Great Ones, in the dimension of dreams. He intends to implore the Great Ones to direct him to the golden city.

Carter has a series of astonishing adventures as he tries to make his way to the Great Ones. From ghoul-infested caverns on a remote island all the way to the moon itself, Carter proceeds on his dangerous quest. The story's most exciting sequence has the ghouls helping Carter escape from the land of giant "gugs" by climbing an outsized staircase with yard-high steps. After some epic encounters with other-worldly beings, not to mention the Great Ones, Carter learns the wondrous city he glimpsed in his dreams is really just "the sum of what you have seen and loved in youth." This conclusion is anticlimactic, perhaps, but charming, and it gives Lovecraft a chance to describe Boston and Providence in some of his most elegiac prose:

> It is the glory of Boston's Hillside roofs and western windows aflame with sunset; of the flower-fragrant

> Common and the great dome on the hill and the tangle
> of gables and chimneys in the violet valley where the
> many-bridged Charles flows drowsily. These things
> you saw, Randolph Carter, when your nurse first
> wheeled you out in the springtime, and they will be the
> last things you will ever see with eyes of memory and
> of love.

Lovecraft captured the basic truth that as people get
older and near death, their distant memories become
more vivid. They often develop longings for the places
of their youth, which time imbues with an added luster.
There are times when the novella seems more nostalgic
than something by the master of dark fantasy, but
Lovecraft's powers of description, and his ability to
create atmosphere and dread, never fail him.

Lovecraft never tried to market either of these works,
and they were not published in his lifetime. He claimed
he simply did not have the energy to retype such lengthy
manuscripts, even though he spent hours and hours
composing letters to his friends.

As his friend Donald Wollheim put it:

> He is one of the most brilliant scholars you're ever
> likely to know in your life. He knows a half-dozen
> languages, has a fine knowledge of many sciences, is
> a very talented writer and poet, and has one of the
> finest brains in the world. The only trouble with him
> is that he lacks *push*, if you know what I mean.
> Otherwise the world would know of him.

It was also in his post-New York period that Lovecraft wrote one of his most famous stories, "The Call of Cthulhu" (1926). In this frightening story, a man learns of a cult that worships old gods from the stars, including the priest Cthulhu. The final and scariest segment of the story takes place on an island-tomb that has risen from the sea, where sailors encounter the gargantuan Cthulhu. Cthulhu had been mentioned in earlier stories, but this was the first of Lovecraft's tales to make major use of the terrifying entity.

What came to be known as "The Cthulhu Mythos" stories propose the theory that Earth was once inhabited by an ancient, alien race of "Elder Gods" or "Great Old Ones" who were expelled or imprisoned by other cosmic forces and are constantly on the brink of a terrifying resurrection. Just as he had once created small imaginary towns in his childhood home, Lovecraft created a whole fictional universe in which these tales would play out. This included weird New England towns (particularly Arkham, Massachusetts) sometimes based on real ones; the Miskatonic University; and the blasphemous *Necronomicon*, an ancient tome that contains forbidden knowledge of the Great Old Ones and how to summon or defeat them.

Not only did these stories influence many writers, some of whom to this day continue to employ the Cthulhu Mythos in their work, they also led many people to mistakenly believe there actually was a book called the *Necronomicon*. The mad Arab, Abdul Alhazred, who supposedly compiled the book, only existed in

Lovecraft's imagination. (Acting out his favorite Arabian Nights stories as a child, Lovecraft had called himself Abdul Alhazred.) Wollheim once wrote a spoof review of the *Necronomicon* as if it actually existed.

"If the Necronomicon legend continues to grow," wrote Lovecraft, "people will end up by believing in it and accusing me of faking when I point out the true origin of the thing!" Several authors have published collections of Lovecraft-inspired works purporting to be the "rediscovered" or "real" *Necronomicon*. All of them, of course, are satirical in nature or literary hoaxes, depending on one's point of view.

Lovecraft's protégé Robert Bloch felt:

> The so-called 'Cthulhu Mythos' represents Lovecraft's chief claim to fame and the stories in which it evolves bring together all of his major influences and interests . . . While imaginary worlds abound in modern fantasy, few of today's writers set their sagas in Poictesme, Perelanda, or Middle-Earth. But stories and novels based on the Mythos continue to proliferate. In terms of imitation and inspiration, Lovecraft may well have had more influence on other writers than any contemporary except Ernest Hemingway.

Over the years, Lovecraft fans have struggled with the pronunciation of "Cthulhu." When asked, Lovecraft would wink and say:

> Authorities seem to differ. Of course it is not a human name at all—having never been designed for

enunciation by the vocal apparatus of homo sapiens. The best approximation one can make is to grunt, bark, or cough the imperfectly-formed syllables of Cluh-Luh with the tip of the tongue firmly affixed to the roof of the mouth. That is, if one is a human being. Directions for other entities are naturally different.

There were other notable works during this productive period. "Pickman's Model" (1926) made use of Lovecraft's knowledge of Boston in a tale of a painting that depicts an attack on a subway station by subterranean creatures. "The Silver Key" (1926) brought back Randolph Carter as an old man who has lost his sense of wonder and ability to dream; he goes back to his youth to reclaim them. "The Strange High House in the Mist" (1926) won first place in an O. Henry short story competition. In *The Colour Out of Space* (1927) the radiation from a life-form inside a meteor causes mutations in plant and animal life. This story was written decades before the post-World War II onslaught of science fiction stories and movies about the negative effects of atomic radiation. None of these Lovecraft classics earned him much money. The payments for his best pulp efforts typically ran from fifty-five dollars to as much as $165. Over his career, he earned an average of about three hundred dollars a year from his fiction.

Despite the lack of financial rewards, Lovecraft was at his creative peak, but there was emotional turmoil lying ahead that would make his artistic achievements seem almost worthless.

Chapter Seven

Ghostwriter

Farnsworth Wright, the new editor of *Weird Tales*, liked Lovecraft's work, as had Edwin Baird, the previous editor. He bought several of his stories when they did not appeal to the editors of other fiction magazines. Wright told Lovecraft he wanted to publish a book of his stories. Lovecraft was delighted by the idea; he felt that in the minds of horror and fantasy fans it would elevate him above the other "hacks" who wrote for *Weird Tales*.

Lovecraft set about deciding which stories would work best in a single volume. He eventually decided to include: "The Outsider," "Arthur Jermyn," "Rats in the Walls," "The Picture in the House," "Pickman's Model," "The Music of Erich Zann," "Dagon," "The Statement of Randolph Carter," and "The Cats of Ulthar." These stories had been written over a number of years and had all been published in *Weird Tales*. Lovecraft also suggested using one of the novellas, such as *The Colour*

Out of Space, which had been published elsewhere. He also suggested a title for the volume: *The Outsider and Other Stories.*

The book was never to appear, though. *Weird Tales* had already published another book and its sales were so disappointing Wright cancelled plans for the Lovecraft volume. Lovecraft's disappointment was somewhat mitigated by the fact that small press publisher W. Paul Cook decided to publish a pamphlet consisting of Lovecraft's "The Shunned House" along with poems by Lovecraft's pal Frank Belknap Long. Cook printed the pamphlet, but it was not bound and distributed until several years later.

G.P. Putnam's Sons and Alfred A. Knopf also rejected a volume of Lovecraft's short stories in the early 1930s. The editor at Putnam's felt the stories lacked subtlety and were all cut from the same grim cloth. Lovecraft bristled at the suggestion that stories in a collection should have varying moods. He blamed "that ass" Farnsworth Wright for the charge of lack of subtlety. Wright had found so many of his stories vague and obtuse that Lovecraft had revised them to be more accessible to the average reader.

In 1928, Lovecraft wrote another story that was destined to become an influential classic: "The Dunwich Horror." Although Lovecraft was not the first "weird" author to exploit the idea of a union between god and human, "The Dunwich Horror" expands upon the concept to achieve a notably scary effect. The creature that results from the union is not only enormous and bizarre, but also invisible. Lovecraft's fascinating descriptions and shuddery prose are at their peak in one of the very first "giant monster" stories.

Lovecraft collected many of the atmospheric details of the story from a trip he took to Wilbraham, Massachusetts, to visit a colleague named Edith Miniter. There he saw the whippoorwills that gathered about an old house, and a huge collection of fireflies over a meadow that he incorporated into "The Dunwich Horror" to great effect. Other details were gleaned from a trip to Bear's Den in Massachusetts, a lonely spot in the woods where there were gorges, waterfalls, and a multitude of caverns. Although Lovecraft had written about sinister caves in many of his stories, this was the first time he had actually entered one.

Fascinated, he looked forward to exploring even larger caves in the future. In late 1928, he traveled south to the Endless Caverns in the Shenandoah Valley of Virginia. He was enthralled; his imagination soared the deeper he descended. "For over an hour I was led spellbound through illimitable gulfs and chasms of elfin beauty and daemonic mystery . . . down, down to the sunless secrets of the gnomes and night-gaunts."

Despite his poverty, Lovecraft did a great deal of traveling in the late 1920s. He lived very frugally, not only because he made little money, but also because he wanted to save for his trips. Sometimes he would go off on a jaunt after receiving a check for a story. His traveling costs were kept low by not going to fancy restaurants and nightclubs as most people did while on vacation. He saved on hotel bills by staying with friends, who usually fed him during the several days of his visit. As Lovecraft was a charming, intelligent, and well-mannered visitor, few people ever complained. Sometimes he went to meet correspondents, on other occasions he traveled in search for antiquities.

In 1927, he traveled to Deerfield, Massachusetts, where he marveled at the "archaic" architecture of the houses. From there he went on to Vermont, where he was charmed by its idyllic quietude and covered bridges. A recluse named Bert G. Akley became the basis of the character of Henry Wentworth Akeley in "The Whisperer in Darkness" (1930). On subsequent trips he also visited Albany, New York, and the Catskill Mountains; Baltimore, Maryland, where he saw Poe's grave; Annapolis, Maryland, to visit the crypt of John Paul Jones; Mt. Vernon, Virginia, the home of George Washington; Philadelphia, Pennsylvania; and Washington, D.C.

In 1929, he lingered in the Poe Shrine with its collection of Poe memorabilia in Richmond, Virginia, and visited Williamsburg, which was then in the midst of being restored to its Colonial period. Lovecraft planned to return when the restoration was complete. He was also fascinated by the Old World charm of Yorktown and Jamestown. With Frank Belknap Long, he went to meet a correspondent named Bernard Austin Dwyer in Kingston, New York. Dwyer put Lovecraft up for several days, after which the author continued on to New Paltz, which to Lovecraft's delight also retained a touch of the early eighteenth century.

A trip he did not enjoy nearly so well was a return to New York City in the spring of 1928. Although Sonia had understood his frantic desire to get out of the city while she was in Ohio, she had now returned to New York and expected him to return to her side. She reminded him he was still her husband. It was one thing for him to stay in Providence while she was halfway across the country, but in her opinion it made little sense for him to do so when she was relatively close by in Brooklyn. Besides, Sonia had saved enough money to open a new hat shop.

Lovecraft never thought of his return to the city he hated as anything more than temporary. He only wanted to please the woman to whom he owed so much. During his stay, he saw more of Frank Belknap Long and other friends than he did of his wife. This brief interlude made it clear to both Sonia and Lovecraft that their marriage had no future. Sonia decided to file for divorce, but there were complications due to the laws in New York at the time, which decreed that a divorce could be granted only if one party were an adulterer or in prison for life.

As this was not the case, Lovecraft had to file for divorce in Rhode Island on the grounds of "desertion." For court purposes, he argued that by not accompanying him to Providence, his wife had deserted *him*. Both Lovecraft and Sonia were well aware that the opposite was true. Lovecraft was irritated by this need for subterfuge. "There is not one modicum of sense in denying divorce to any couple that mutually desire it," he complained. Naturally, Lovecraft hated the idea of alimony, although Sonia did not expect any. "Alimony is a relique [sic] of obsolescent economics and a source of ridiculous extortion," he protested.

Despite his fondness for Sonia, Lovecraft was happy to be rid of his wife. "With a wife of the same temperament as my mother and aunts," Lovecraft noted, "I would probably have been able to reconstruct a type of domestic life not unlike that of Angell St. days." Sonia later married a man named Nathaniel Davis and moved to California. Like many members of Lovecraft's inner circle, she wrote a memoir of him some years after his death.

As his short story writing brought in little money, Lovecraft expanded his coffers by ghostwriting. Previously, he had revised stories for colleagues at no charge, but it took so much of his time that he decided that he should be well paid for it. "Revision is really not only as hard as original writing, but (for me, at least) actually *harder*," he told one potential client. "It takes just as much (or more) of my time and energy to give a tale a thorough re-writing as to create one of my own." For this reason, he explained, he could not perform any revisions if payment was dependent on the story being accepted. "I could just as easily compose an original tale and have an equal chance of *all* the proceeds."

He was also not interested in collaborating and sharing the credit for a story. "Collaboration in serious writing does not pay anybody who has an adequate stock of original ideas. The only ones for whom it is at all profitable are the commercial formula-experts who can effortlessly adapt any idea to a saleable hack framework." Nevertheless Lovecraft did work up stories based on synopses or premises provided by others.

Some clients, such as Harry Houdini, did little more than give Lovecraft a bare outline of a story, or a wisp of a premise. He did so much work for such clients as Zealia Brown Bishop and Hazel Heald that the results were often much more Lovecraft than Bishop or Heald. Lovecraft claimed that Bishop's "The Curse of Yig," which was published by *Weird Tales*, was seventy-five percent Lovecraft. In some stories, Lovecraft would use elements of the Cthulhu Mythos. The only reason most of these stories are not simply considered works by Lovecraft is because he wrote them to order and considered them inferior to his "solo" stories. When it was confirmed after his death that Lovecraft had been the partial or complete author of these stories, some of them that had been originally rejected by *Weird Tales* were then published by the magazine.

Lovecraft was disheartened that so many people still expected him to work on their stories for free. "I always like to help a fellow-struggler along when I can, but correcting stories and poems is too exhausting and time-consuming a process to undertake lightly."

Lovecraft found he could make more money by writing his own stories than by ghost-writing others. When sold to *Weird Tales*, "The Whisperer in Darkness" (1930) netted him $350, the most money he had ever received for a single story. Of course, "The Whisperer in Darkness" was almost novella length. One of Lovecraft's most frightening and absorbing stories, it deals with the intentions of unfriendly aliens connected to Pluto, which had been recently discovered by C.W. Tombaugh. Like some of Lovecraft's other stories, "The Whisperer in Darkness" is a horror-fantasy tale that makes use of science-fiction concepts such as a "disembodied brain machine."

In late 1929, in the span of just one week, Lovecraft wrote a series of thirty-six macabre sonnets, which he called "Fungi from Yuggoth." Later, he apparently decided to use the name of the mysterious world in his sonnets for the alien name of the newly-discovered planet, Pluto. He planned to use some of the other ideas and imagery of the sonnets in his stories as well. Although Lovecraft wrote poems off and on throughout his life, he was always best known for his fiction.

In 1930, Lovecraft continued his travels. His first destination was Charleston, South Carolina, which he found "the best-preserv'd colonial city of any size, without exception, that I have ever encounter'd. Virtually *everything* is just as it was in the reign of George the Third." He especially loved the proliferation of wrought-iron gates and balconies, and the "luxurious" gardens surrounded by high walls. He sailed to Sullivan's Island in Charleston's harbor, which Poe had used as the setting for several scenes of his story "The Gold Bug." "It gave me a thrill to visit in person a region familiar to me in literature for above thirty years," he wrote.

Lovecraft was so impressed by Quebec City, Canada, he wrote a travelogue in its honor. *(Courtesy of the Library of Congress.)*

Later that year, he again braved New York City, where he visited museums with old friend Samuel Loveman and others. At Loveman's home one night, the doorbell rang and there was Hart Crane. Crane had become a celebrated poet, and Lovecraft was a great admirer of his epic poem, *The Bridge*. Lovecraft was saddened to see that Crane, despite his success, was a nearly dissolute alcoholic. "At the very crest of his fame," Lovecraft noted, "he is on the verge of psychological, physical, and financial disintegration, with no certainty of ever having the inspiration to write a major work of literature again." Even though Crane was much more widely known and admired than Lovecraft was at the time, Lovecraft could not envy him. Crane committed suicide two years later.

Four months after visiting New York, Lovecraft left the United States for the first time in his life to travel to

Quebec, Canada. He tended to see each new city he visited as being even more spectacular than the last, but he was genuinely bowled over by Quebec. "All my former standards of urban beauty must be abandoned after my sight of Quebec," he raved. "It hardly belongs to the world of prosaic reality at all."

He adored the winding, mysterious streets, the old world style architecture, and most of all, the leisurely pace. Smitten, he went back to Quebec twice more in the next few years. He even wrote a travelogue entitled *A Description of the Town of Quebeck* [sic] (1931). His passion for the city is apparent in the fact that the travelogue, a love valentine to Quebec, is longer than any of Lovecraft's novellas.

Lovecraft's fiction output was not proceeding as easily, however. In the period of 1929 to 1930, he wrote only one story, "The Whisperer in Darkness." Part of the trouble was the rejection of his volume of short stories by the major firms made him doubt himself. Maybe he was not really any better a writer than the "hacks" who were usually published in *Weird Tales*. This loss of confidence temporarily kept him away from writing more stories.

Chapter Eight

The Final Years

Lovecraft's confidence was restored in 1931. He returned to fiction with an impressive spurt of creativity that produced one long story and one novella that are among his very best. In both "The Shadow over Innsmouth" and *At the Mountains of Madness*, Lovecraft demonstrates his gift for creating a mood of dread that is almost palpable. Also much in evidence is his impressive ability to concoct fantastic locations that do not exist on Earth, but that come fully alive in the mind of the reader. The seaside town of Innsmouth and the abandoned city behind the Mountains of Madness seem as real to readers as any place they might actually visit.

At the Mountains of Madness, arguably Lovecraft's greatest novella, relates the strange things that befall an expedition to the Antarctic. Some of the members enter the Mountains of Madness and bring out several seemingly dead creatures that might be animal or vegetable. When the rest of the expedition finally arrives, after a terrible storm, all but one of the men in camp have been slaughtered. Most of the strange creatures are missing.

Behind the gigantic mountain range, the narrator and a man named Danforth discover a lost city, which predates human history. Inside this city—which is described down to the minute details of its weird architecture and its many tunnels and levels—the duo finds evidence that the creatures have come back to life. They are returning to the underground areas after abandoning the city eons ago. In a terrifying moment, the two men are chased by an enormous powerful presence that Lovecraft likens to a subway train barreling down a track.

Lovecraft had still more surprises up his sleeve. He not only fabricated the abandoned city; he also related the entire earthly history of this star-spawned race. It once dominated the land and seas and fought a war against another group of alien entities. He described what led to the race leaving the city and to the debasement of its art and culture. Influenced by Poe's "Arthur Gordon Pym," this novella even incorporates the phrase "*Tekeli-li*," which the natives cry in Poe's story. He also referred on occasion to such elements of the Cthulhu Mythos as the *Necronomicon*.

Lovecraft insisted not a sentence, word, or comma be changed in his stories. Therefore, he was enraged when the copy-editor for *Astounding Stories* made a multitude of what he thought were unnecessary revisions to his story. "My *Mountains of Madness* was atrociously and injuriously mangled toward the end," he ranted, "and the style-sheet determiner of *Astounding* is an absolute ass for capitalising words like 'moon' and 'moonlight,' for changing words like 'dinosaurs' to "dinosauria,' and for illiterately altering 'subterrene' to 'subterrane'—the latter word having no existence as an adjective!"

By 1931, Lovecraft wrote about one story a year for the next six years. He had resigned himself to being, in his own eyes, a minor writer whose work would be forgotten soon after his death: "By the standards of real literature, I simply don't exist," he wrote, "and that is equally true of all the routine hacks who fill the pulp magazines. We are the most negligible of small fry, and anyone who mistakes us for real authors is simply wasting his esteem. If you want to see real artists in fantasy, look outside the magazine field—at Dunsany, Blackwood, Poe, Machen, de la Mare, Bierve, the late M. R. James, et cetera."

He thought the greatest horror story of all time was Algernon Blackwood's "The Willows" (1906). Looking at the writers of the period who were the most highly respected—Theodore Dreiser, for instance, whom Lovecraft admired—he noticed they all wrote realistic books and were adept at incisive characterization. These were not Lovecraft's strong points. He had little talent for realistic fiction. He blamed this deficiency on his shyness and the ill health he suffered early in life. "I don't know enough about life to be an effective exponent of it," he wrote. "I don't know what different kinds of people do and think and feel and say . . . I have absolutely nothing to say where actual, unvarnished life is concerned." Lovecraft's haughty provincialism, and his refusal to even try to understand people who were different from him, left him isolated and insulated in more ways than one. Only later in life did he admit certain of his attitudes had impeded his growth as an artist.

Lovecraft stubbornly clung to his insistence that "real" writers did not worry about commercial matters. It is ironic that he did this even as he decried the fact that in the eyes of the literary establishment he was not a "real" writer. Friends of his argued with him that there was nothing wrong in writing commercial fiction for sustenance and doing more artistic work on the side. In truth, Lovecraft was embarrassed by his lack of success and ambition and made excuses for it any way he could.

It was again often difficult for Lovecraft to find the energy to write, and thinking about his status in the world of letters only depressed him further. When he did take up pen and paper, it was more often to write the voluminous letters that he sent to anyone and everyone.

In his letters, Lovecraft spells out at great length the details of his trips, worries, prejudices, and attitudes toward life and the cosmos. While this might be seen as another sign of his self-absorption, he was also a lonely man who cherished the replies he received and the contacts he made. His many efforts to help and advise his fellow writers also indicated a nature that was not entirely selfish. Ever practical, he also knew there was always the possibility he might receive an invitation to visit and stay with one of his correspondents. Lovecraft became a freeloader partly out of necessity and partly because he truly believed he made a fascinating guest.

Lovecraft exchanged so many letters with his correspondents that even the ones he never met face to face became genuine friends. Some of his friends were professional writers and others were aspiring writers who became his protégés. His most frequent correspondents during the final years included Robert H. Barlow, Kenneth Sterling, Robert Bloch, Henry Kuttner, Frank Belknap Long, E. Hoffmann Price, August W. Derleth, Donald Wandrei, Clark Ashton Smith, Robert E. Howard, Fritz Lieber, and Miss C.L. Moore. All of these were writers, several quite successful, except for Barlow.

In his forties, Lovecraft also corresponded with a young man named Willis Conover, who edited the small press publication *Fantasy Magazine*. Conover even had the nerve to reject Lovecraft's story "The Tree." "It isn't nearly so good a representation of your work," he wrote Lovecraft. "May I relay it to some less fortunate fan-magazine editor who lacks and wants material by you?" When Lovecraft, at the time forty-five or six, sent Conover some pictures of himself, the boy was struck by the fact that the deadly serious Lovecraft looked older in his youth than in recent photos.

Protégé Robert Bloch later became famous as the author of *Psycho*, which was filmed by Alfred Hitchcock in 1960. Bloch sent Conover a parody entitled "A Visit with H.P. Lovecraft" which depicts Lovecraft as "a little old man with a long white beard." Invited to dinner, Bloch is surprised to see there is nothing on the table. "I thought you invited me for a meal," he says. "I did," replies Lovecraft, "you're the meal." Lovecraft loved the story and wrote, "I seldom eat people alive except for Sunday dinner."

Lovecraft liked and admired Robert E. Howard, the creator of Conan the Barbarian, even though he felt he was only of average intelligence. Howard "is original and distinctive in thought and expression," he noted. His nickname for Howard was "Two-Gun," and he was saddened to hear of Howard's suicide in 1936. Lovecraft had contemplated suicide several times throughout his lifetime, but it always seemed to be others around him who finally took that irrevocable step.

Lovecraft warned his protégés not to bother delving too much into magic and folklore for their stories. "You will undoubtedly find all this stuff very disappointing. It is flat, childish, pompous, and unconvincing—merely a record of human childishness and gullibility in past ages. Any good fiction writer can think up 'records of primal horror,' which surpass in imaginative force any occult production which has sprung from genuine credulousness." In other words, Lovecraft felt a writer should just make it up.

Lovecraft continued to travel. In addition to his return trips to Quebec, he visited St. Augustine and Key West in Florida. Lovecraft found Miami a bit too modern for his taste. In Florida, his hosts included the forty-nine-year-old writer Henry S. Whitehead, a church rector who invited members of his boys' club over to hear Lovecraft tell impromptu versions of some of his stories. According to Lovecraft, Whitehead so enjoyed his company he did not want him to leave.

His other Floridian host of note was correspondent Robert H. Barlow, who lived in a town near Jacksonville. Barlow was the sixteen-year-old son of a retired army colonel. Nowadays, if a man in his forties showed up on a doorstep saying he was a friend of a teenaged member of the family, suspicions might be raised. There is nothing to indicate that Lovecraft's relationship with Barlow was anything but a friendship, however, Barlow's family seems to have recognized Lovecraft was lonely and needed a place to stay.

Lovecraft found Barlow to be wise beyond his years. He grew close to him and to members of his family during his visits. Barlow eventually built a cabin on his family's property, where Lovecraft would stay for months at a time. Lovecraft made Barlow his literary executor. After working in Mexico as an anthropologist, Barlow killed himself in 1951, at the age of thirty-three.

Whether traveling, staying with friends, or at home in Providence, Lovecraft rarely had much money to spend. The largest check he ever received was $595 for the sale of both "The Shadow out of Time" and *At the Mountains of Madness* to *Astounding Stories*. He knew his income to be "sadly microscopic." In addition to his occasional writing and many revision assignments, he tried to "whip into shape a textbook on English usage for the head of a school in Washington. If I didn't piece out by slowly using up the last few dregs of my existing property . . . I wouldn't be eating very much." There came the possibility of employment in Vermont, but Lovecraft had to turn this down due to a strange (possibly psychosomatic) condition he had, which made him pass out if exposed for too long a time to extremely cold weather. This affliction even inspired one of his most bizarre stories, "Cool Air" (1926).

Although other stories and characters that were first brought to life in pulp magazines, such as Doc Savage, were used for motion pictures, Lovecraft did not sell anything to Hollywood in his lifetime. He did not have a high opinion of the horror films he saw. "All of the so-called weird cinemas are infantile and unconvincing—at least, all I've ever seen," he wrote. While Lovecraft had advised his fellow horror writers to avoid use of folklore and conventional sources on magic, the movies focused almost exclusively on well-known monsters and curses. Lovecraft so detested the horror film reviews in *Fantasy Magazine* by Forrest J. Ackerman, which he thought were overenthusiastic, that the magazine's publisher, Willis Conover, finally agreed to replace Ackerman with another reviewer.

Although many authors and screenwriters over the years have used his ideas without giving him credit, Lovecraft would probably have disowned the official film adaptations of his stories. These include *Die, Monster, Die* (1965), a dumbed-down version of *The Colour Out of Space*; *The Dunwich Horror* (1965); *From Beyond; The Unnameable* (1988); and *The Unnameable 2:*

The Statement of Randolph Carter (2000). The last three were silly, distorted versions of lesser-known Lovecraft stories. When *The Case of Charles Dexter Ward* was filmed in 1963, it was released under the title *The Haunted Palace* and promoted as an adaptation of the poem of that title by Edgar Allan Poe. Although the film conformed to the basic premise of Lovecraft's novella, it had little to do with Lovecraft and nothing whatsoever to do with Poe.

Of the half-dozen or so stories Lovecraft wrote in his forties, most would agree that the best is "The Shadow Out of Time" (1934-1935). This profoundly frightening and imaginative piece grew out of the idea of a man finding, as Lovecraft put it, "a specimen of his own handwriting in English" on ancient papyrus while excavating some ruins. Lovecraft almost tossed this idea aside, suggesting writer-friend Clark Ashton Smith use it in one of his own stories. Luckily, Smith declined. Other Lovecraft tales of his late period include "The Thing on the Doorstep" (1935), "The Haunter of the Dark" (1935), the disturbing and effective "Dreams in the Witch-House" (1932), and Lovecraft's final work, "The Evil Clergyman" (1937).

Lovecraft had to cut short his travels during the summer of 1932, when his Aunt Lillian became seriously ill. Mrs. Clark, who was seventy-six, had suffered for years from severe arthritis and other ailments. Finally, there came, as Lovecraft termed it, "an unexpected weakening and collapse of the general organic system." Although Lovecraft rushed home after receiving a telegram from his Aunt Annie, Lillian Clark had fallen into a coma by the time he returned. She died the following day, July 3. Lillian had been such an important part of his life for so many years that her death hit him almost as hard as when his mother passed away.

The following spring, Lovecraft moved from the apartment he had shared with Lillian into a new place with his Aunt Annie at 66 College Street. He was delighted to be living in a genuine Colonial house for the first time in his life. A friend of Annie's who had wanted her to move in upstairs as soon as it was vacated occupied the bottom of the house. Although Lovecraft told friends that the chief reason for the move was to save money, he could not bear living alone. The rent was the same as at 10 Barnes Street, although he now had two rooms instead of one.

By this time, he had finally rejected the class-consciousness that permeated his aunt's generation. He was annoyed at her when a nice family moved into the apartment below them (the friend having moved elsewhere), and she was appalled that neither she nor her friends "knew" them. Lovecraft was completely unsympathetic to his aunt's complaint that the newcomers had no social standing in Providence.

Lovecraft's intolerant views toward other cultures and races underwent a transformation in the early to mid-1930s. He did not discard all his prejudices, but he did become more open-minded. He had praised Adolf Hitler during his rise to power, but that began to change after Hitler became chancellor of Germany in 1933. He took a particularly dim view of the party's book burnings, during which members made bonfires of books counter to their philosophies. As the Nazis began to force artists to create works extolling Nazi Party values, rather than their own vision, he grew incensed. He knew his own bizarre muse could never have served up propaganda for a political party.

A short residence in Germany by one of his friends strengthened Lovecraft's belief that the Nazi persecutions were wrong. Alice Sheppard, a retired teacher, left for Germany in August of 1936, planning to stay three years. She returned soon afterwards, bringing first hand accounts of the Nazi's cruelties against Jewish citizens. Lovecraft was appalled, and for the first time in his life, wrote in support of Jewish art.

"The general Jewish question has its perplexing cultural aspects, but the biologically unsound Nazi attitude offers no solution," he wrote. "What is more, it is equally silly to *belittle* even the admittedly hybrid art of Judaeo-Germans or Judaeo-Americans. It may not represent genuine German or American feelings, but it

Following the death of his Aunt Lillian, Lovecraft moved to 66 College Street, where he lived with his Aunt Annie.
(Courtesy of Brown University.)

at least has a right to stand on its own feet as a frankly exotic or composite product–which may well excel much of our own art in intrinsic quality."

Just as surprising a turnaround was Lovecraft's admiration for President Franklin D. Roosevelt and his New Deal economic programs. The stock market had lost eighty percent of its value after the crash of 1929, which ushered in the Great Depression. Roosevelt's New Deal set up work programs, price controls, minimum wages, and social welfare programs for the poor and disabled. Lovecraft called Roosevelt a "gentleman" and considered his efforts compatible with the graciousness the wealthy often extend to the poor. This new-found compassion was a far cry from the contempt that Lovecraft had so often expressed toward all those he considered beneath him. In 1937, Lovecraft attended a New Deal rally and extravagantly praised a rabbi who served as the main speaker.

"I can well imagine the polite Nazis of Wall St. cursing him as a blasphemous non-Aryan intellectual!" Lovecraft wrote.

There was another reason for Lovecraft's new tolerance. As he put it, "The man of science, artist, or philosopher who is not a good money-maker is classed with the shiftless and consigned to suffering and extermination. All values but material values, apparently, are non-existent for hardy upholders of 'our historic pioneer Americanism.' "

As a poor man, Lovecraft knew he too had no "social standing," and he always bristled at the suggestion—

prevalent then as now—that a man should be judged by how aggressively he pursued money and success. This was always a sensitive area for him since colleagues suggested he would have been much better off if he had possessed a healthier dose of ambition in his veins.

Still, Lovecraft was not completely freed from his ego and self-righteousness. "I must write my autobiography some day," he told one correspondent.

> Every mediocre, uninteresting person of late seems absolutely determined to write his autobiography, especially if he has done nothing whatsoever to warrant it. I must be pompous and colourful, and supply the element of dramatic interest where life has failed to supply it . . . Lifelong indolence and nearly lifelong ill-health have made my annals as short and simple as those of the class who subsist on W.T. [*Weird Tales*] cheques!

Lovecraft eventually began working on his memoir, but did not live long enough to write more than a brief autobiographical sketch he titled, "Some Notes on a Nonentity." Asked what he would do if he knew he only had one hour to live, he replied he would write down instructions for the disposition of his possessions. Ironically, at a later point, he did just that. In the early weeks of 1937, he took many walks through the woods of Providence and actually discovered some areas he had never before encountered. "Only two or three miles from the city's heart," he exclaimed, "and yet in the primal rural New England of the first colonists!" He would write lovingly of the many cats he would encounter on his walks, as he always had a special feeling for felines, as was made clear in his tale "The Cats of Ulthar" (1920).

In late 1936, Wilfred Blanch Talman, a writer-friend, spoke to editors at the publishing house of William Morrow on Lovecraft's behalf. Talman felt Lovecraft's morale, self-esteem, and financial situation would be boosted by an advance for a novel, and urged him to put together a proposal for them to look at. Earlier that year, a book version of "The Shadow over Innsmouth" had been issued by a small company, Visionary Publishing of Pennsylvania, but this would be a brand new project from a major New York publishing house.

Lovecraft was excited by the prospect, but developed increasingly severe stomach complaints in late 1936 and early 1937. He had had "indigestion" for quite some time but had not taken it seriously. He did not have the money to spend on doctors and often put off visiting them. Things finally got so bad that his physician called in a stomach specialist. The diagnosis was grim—intestinal cancer and kidney disease.

He reported on his condition to Talman in uncharacteristically clipped sentences, necessitated by his condition: "Am in constant pain, take only liquid food, and so bloated with gas that I can't lie down. Spend all time in chair propped with pillows, and can read or write only a few minutes at a time. Taking 3 medicines at once . . . you and the firm are unbelievably kind and liberal—but what can a guy do when he hardly has strength enough to walk across the room?"

In spite of the pain—and the fact that he thought it unlikely he would recover—he took the time to wish Talman well on his endeavors and to offer advice on the other man's career. In early March, he sent back a postcard he had received from Willis Conover with the scribbled words, "Am very ill and likely to be so for a long time."

Lovecraft was admitted to Jane Brown Memorial Hospital in Providence on March 10, 1937. Willis Conover received a postcard from Lovecraft's aunt dated March 15: "This morning my beloved nephew Howard Phillips Lovecraft died after five days in the hospital. I am sorry I have not written these past days but my mind and heart and hands have been so full. I was with Howard all of yesterday afternoon and I saw how weak he was but I tried to still have hope." He was forty-six.

After his death, Lovecraft's loyal friends and admirers struggled to get a collection of his work into print. It was not easy. Finally, the writers August Derleth and Donald Wandrei formed their own company, Arkham House, and published *The Outsider and Others*. There continued to be problems getting out subsequent volumes when Lovecraft's surviving aunt, Annie, demanded royalties and Derleth and Wandrei entered into legal battles of their own. The suicide of Robert H. Barlow, Lovecraft's literary executor, further complicated matters. Today, major publishing houses put out many different volumes of Lovecraft's collected stories and novellas. This has been the case since his "rediscovery" around the 1970s.

In his lifetime, Lovecraft encouraged such writers as Derleth, Robert Bloch, Clark Ashton Smith, Frank Belknap Long, Robert E. Howard, Fritz Lieber, and others. He also influenced generations of writers thereafter, with Lovecraftian themes appearing in the work of Ray Bradbury, Richard Matheson, Rod Serling, and even mainstream authors such as Joyce Carol Oates. In 1990, an anthology entitled *Lovecraft's Legacy* marked the one hundredth anniversary of his birth. Edited by Robert E. Weinberg and Martin H. Greenberg, the book contained new stories based on the Cthulhu Mythos by some of the most prominent horror writers of the time, including Ed Gorman, Brian Lumley, Gary Brandner, Chet Williamson, and Graham Masterton.

Despite his dissatisfaction with his career and literary standing, and his personal problems, Lovecraft made many lasting friendships through his life. He personally touched the lives of dozens of associates, and hundreds of thousands more were infected with devilish delight by his stories. He wrote a handful of gripping works that for decades have remained some of the very best examples of their genre.

"Now that time has given us some perspective on his work," says horror writer Stephen King, "I think it is beyond doubt that H.P. Lovecraft has yet to be surpassed as the Twentieth Century's greatest practitioner of the classic horror tale."

Major Works

NOTE: Important works are marked with an asterisk.
*Dagon 1917
*The Tomb 1917
Psychopompos 1917
Polaris 1918
Beyond the Wall of Sleep 1919
The Doom that Came to Sarnath 1919
*The Statement of Randolph Carter 1919
The White Ship 1919
Arthur Jermyn (The White Ape) 1920
The Cats of Ulthar 1920
Celephais 1920
From Beyond 1920
The Picture in the House 1920
The Temple 1920
The Terrible Old Man 1920
The Tree 1920
The Moon-Bog 1920
*The Music of Erich Zann 1921
The Nameless City 1921
The Other Gods 1921
The Outsider 1921
The Quest of Iranon 1921
*Herbert West: Reanimator 1922
*The Hound 1922
Hypnos 1922
*The Lurking Fear 1922
The Festival 1923
*The Rats in the Walls 1923
The Unnameable 1923
Imprisoned with the Pharaohs 1924
*The Shunned House 1924
*He 1925

*The Horror at Red Hook 1925
In the Vault 1925
*The Call of Cthulhu 1926
Cool Air 1926
*Pickman's Model 1926
The Silver Key 1926
The Strange High House in the Mist 1926
Dream Quest of Unknown Kadath (novella) 1927
The Colour Out of Space 1927
Supernatural Horror in Literature 1927
The Case of Charles Dexter Ward (novel) 1928
*The Dunwich Horror 1928

*The Whisperer in Darkness 1920
*The Shadow Over Innsmouth 1931
At the Mountains of Madness (novella) 1931
*The Dreams in the Witch-House 1932
Through the Gates of the Silver Key 1932
The Thing on the Doorstep 1933
*The Shadow Out of Time 1934
*The Haunter of the Dark 1935
The Evil Clergyman 1937

Timeline

1890   Howard Phillips Lovecraft is born on August 20.

1893   Lovecraft's father is institutionalized; he and his mother move in with his maternal grandparents.

1904   Grandfather dies; family forced to move.

1908   Suffers nervous breakdown that lasts for five years.

1915   Begins publishing *The Conservative*, an amateur journal.

1916   Appointed vice president of the United Amateur Press Association (UAPA).

1917   Becomes president of the UAPA.

1920   Edits the UAPA newsletter.

1921   Mother dies; meets Sonia Greene.

1922   Visits New York City for the first time.

1924   Marries Sonia Greene.

1926   Separates from Sonia Greene; returns to Providence to live with his Aunt Lillian.

1932   Death of Aunt Lillian.

1933   Moves in with Aunt Annie.

1937   Dies on March 10.

Sources

CHAPTER ONE: The Living Death
p. 9, "I don't find a single mark . . ." Lovecraft to Maurice W. Moe, April 5, 1931.

p. 12, "became the center of [his] entire universe . . ." Ibid.

p. 13, "a serene, quiet lady . . ." Lovecraft to Rheinhart Kleiner, November 16, 1916.

p. 16, "I never had the slightest shadow of belief in the supernatural." Ibid.

p. 17, "This pursuit of science . . . " Ibid.

p. 19, "There was a kind of intoxication . . ." Lovecraft to J. Vernon Shea, November 11, 1933.

p. 22, "I felt I had lost my entire adjustment . . ." Ibid., February 4, 1934.

p. 23, "And yet certain elements . . ." Ibid.

CHAPTER TWO: Out of the Shadows
p. 26, "I could hardly bear to see or speak to . . ." Lovecraft to R.H. Barlow, April 10, 1934.

p. 27, "I simply prefer to have intimacy . . ." Lovecraft to Rheinhart Kleiner, December 4, 1918.

p. 29, "The atmosphere is wholly . . ." *UAPA: Exponent of Amateur Journalism.* (Elroy, Wisc.: E.E. Ericson, 1915.)

p. 30, "I obtained a new will to live . . ." H.P. Lovecraft, "What Amateurdom and I Have Done for Each Other" *Boys' Herald,* 1937.

p. 32, "Englishmen and Germans . . ." L. Sprague de Camp, *Lovecraft: A Biography* (New York: Ballantine Books, 1975), 97.

p. 34, "I am done with Dunn!" Lovecraft to Alfred Galpin, August 29, 1918.

p. 35, "most irregular" Lovecraft to Reinhart Kleiner, May 23, 1917.

p. 35, "killed or cured" Ibid., August 27, 1917.

p. 35, "It is not flattering to be reminded . . ." Ibid., December 23, 1917.

p. 35, "any work requiring . . ." Ibid.

p. 36, "In earlier tales he often relied . . ." Robert Bloch, "Heritage of Horror," *The Best of H.P. Lovecraft,* 13.

p. 37, "some little rusticities . . ." Lovecraft to Alfred Galpin, January 1920.

CHAPTER THREE: Sonia

p. 42, "If she is determined to blow de coin . . ." Lovecraft to Maurice W. Moe, June 21, 1922.

p. 42, "Mme. Greene is certainly a person . . ." Lovecraft to Rheinhart Kleiner, September 21, 1921.

p. 46, "Reg'lar author 'n' everything . . ." Lovecraft to Maurice W. Moe, May 18, 1922.

p. 48, "Out of the waters it rose . . ." Ibid.

p. 49, "flapper" Ibid.

p. 49, "pert, spoiled, and ultra-independent . . ." Ibid.

p. 49, "an exquisite boy of twenty . . ." Ibid.

p. 49, "a small world of magic . . ." Ibid.

p. 50, "A bastard mess of stewing mongrel flesh . . ." Ibid.

p. 52, "What I need is the constant company . . ." Lovecraft to Lillian D. Clark, August 4, 1922.

p. 53, "As I viewed this . . ." Ibid., September 29, 1922.

p. 54, "General Washington could tomorrow . . ." Lovecraft to Rheinhart Kleiner, January 11, 1923.

CHAPTER FOUR: Parkside Avenue

p. 58, "too horrible for the tender sensibilities . . ." Lovecraft to Frank Belknap Long, November 8, 1923.

p. 58, "My criticism of the tale is not . . ." Willis Conover and H.P. Lovecraft, *Lovecraft at Last.* (Arlington, Va: Carrollton-Clark, 1975), 223.

p. 58, "Only a cynic can create horror . . ." Lovecraft to Edwin Baird, September 1923.

p. 60, "would come not as a burden but . . ." Lovecraft to Lillian D. Clark, March 9, 1924.

p. 62, "*Place de la Guillotine* . . ." Ibid.

p. 62, "careless scrawl" Ibid.

p. 62, "Truly a most practical and industrious . . ." Ibid.

p. 63, "The invalidism and seclusion of my earlier . . ." Conover and Lovecraft, *Lovecraft at Last*, 226.

p. 64, "I lack the magnetism or brass . . ." Lovecraft to Lillian D. Clark, August 1, 1924.

p. 65, "a weary and . . ." Ibid., September 29, 1924.

p. 66, "utter and poignant charm" Ibid.

p. 66, "All the Italian squalor was faded . . ." Ibid.

p. 66, "By the time we reached city hall . . ." Ibid.

p. 66, "She never knew when I came back . . ." Lovecraft to James F. Norton, May 6, 1924.

CHAPTER FIVE: The Horrors of Red Hook

p. 71, "Only later was I to learn . . ." Lovecraft to Bernard Austin Dwyer, March 26, 1927.

p. 73, "The mass of contemporary Jews . . ." Lovecraft to Lillian D. Clark, January 11, 1926.

p. 74, "unscientific extremist" Lovecraft to J. Vernon Shea, September 15, 1933.

p. 74, "I wouldn't for the world . . ." Lovecraft to Robert H. Barlow, March 16, 1935.

p. 74, "If Lovecraft was a racist . . ." Bloch, "Heritage of Horror," 6.

p. 75, "I can see myself . . . with an actual income . . ." Lovecraft to Lillian D. Clark, May 28, 1925.

p. 77, "A gentleman should always be attired . . ." Ibid., October, 24, 1925.

p. 77, "less repulsive and mongrel . . ." Ibid., April 21, 1925.

CHAPTER SIX: Creative Peak

p. 79, "Each financial shortcoming . . ." Lovecraft to Lillian D. Clark, December 22, 1925.

p. 79, "devotion which can accept this . . ." Ibid.

p. 80, "found such a prospect . . ." Lovecraft to Maurice W. Moe, July 2, 1929.

p. 81, "I haven't a doubt but that matrimony . . ." Ibid.

p. 81, "New York is dead . . ." Lovecraft to Donald Wandrei, February 10, 1927.

p. 81, "The 'aesthetes' of New York . . ." Ibid.

p. 82, "Not even the threat of damnation . . ." Ibid.

p. 82, "The skyline, the sunsets . . ." Lovecraft to Frank Belknap Long, May 1, 1926.

p. 82, "Providence is part of me . . ." Lovecraft to Lillian D. Clark, March 29, 1926.

p. 85, "He is one of the most brilliant scholars . . ." Conover and Lovecraft, *Lovecraft at Last*, 86.

p. 87, "If the Necronomicon legend . . ." Ibid., 103.

p. 87, "The so-called 'Cthulhu Mythos' represents . . ." Bloch, "A Heritage of Horror," 6.

p. 87, "Authorities seem to differ . . ." Conover and Lovecraft, *Lovecraft at Last*, 77.

CHAPTER SEVEN: Ghostwriter

p. 90, "that ass" Lovecraft to J. Vernon Shea, August 7, 1931.

p. 91, "For over an hour I was led spellbound . . ." Lovecraft to Zealia Bishop, May 1, 1928.

p. 93, "There is not one modicum of sense . . ." Lovecraft to Maurice W. Moe, July 2, 1929.

p. 94, "Alimony is a relique . . ." Ibid.

p. 94, "With a wife of the same temperament . . ." Ibid.

p. 94, "Revision is really not only as hard . . ." Lovecraft to Richard F. Seawright, August 25, 1933.

p. 94, "Collaboration in serious writing . . ." Conover and Lovecraft, *Lovecraft at Last*, 99.

p. 95, "I always like to help . . ." Ibid., 137.

p. 96, "the best-preserv'd colonial city . . ." Lovecraft to Elizabeth Toldridge, May 29, 1929.

p. 96, "It gave me a thrill to visit in person . . ." Ibid.

p. 97, "At the very crest of his fame . . ." Lovecraft to Lillian D. Clark, May 24, 1930.

p. 98, "All my former standards of urban beauty . . ." Lovecraft to Elizabeth Toldridge, September 1930.

CHAPTER EIGHT: The Final Years

p. 100, "My *Mountains of Madness* was atrociously . . ." Conover and Lovecraft, *Lovecraft at Last*, 55.

p. 101, "By the standards of real literature . . ." Ibid., 88.

p. 101, "I don't know enough about life . . ." Lovecraft to E. Hoffmann Price, August 15, 1934.

p. 103, "It isn't nearly so good . . ." Conover and Lovecraft, *Lovecraft at Last*.

p. 104, "a little old man with a long white beard." Ibid., 52-53.

p. 104, "is original and distinctive in thought . . ." Lovecraft to Kenneth Sterling, December 14, 1935.

p. 104, "You will undoubtedly find all this stuff . . ." Conover and Lovecraft, *Lovecraft at Last*, 33.

p. 105, "sadly microscopic" Ibid., 99.

p. 105, "whip into shape a textbook . . ." Ibid.

p. 106, "All of the so-called weird cinemas . . ." Ibid.,73.

p. 107, "a specimen of his own handwriting . . ." Lovecraft to E. Hoffmann Price, November 18, 1934.

p. 107, "an unexpected weakening and collapse . . ." Lovecraft to Maurice W. Moe, July 12, 1932.

p. 109, "The general Jewish question . . ." L. Sprague de Camp, *Lovecraft: A Biography* (New York: Ballantine Books, 1975), 401.

p. 110, "I can well imagine . . ." Ibid., 402.

p. 110, "The man of science, artist, or philosopher . . ." Lovecraft to C.L. Moore, October 1936.

p. 111, "I must write my autobiography some day . . ." Conover and Lovecraft, *Lovecraft at Last*, 201.

p. 111, "Only two or three miles from the city's heart . . ." Lovecraft to James F. Morton, circa 1937.

p. 112, "Am in constant pain . . ." Lovecraft to Wilfred Blanch Talman, February 28, 1937.

p. 113, "Am very ill and likely to be so . . ." Conover and Lovecraft, *Lovecraft at Last*, 244.

p. 113, "This morning my beloved nephew . . ." Ibid., 254.

p. 114, "Now that time has given us some perspective . . ." Stephen King endorsement for *The Best of H.P. Lovecraft*.

Bibliography

Bleiler, E.F., introduction to *Supernatural Horror in Literature*, by H.P. Lovecraft. New York: Dover, 1973.

Bloch, Robert, introduction to *The Best of H.P. Lovecraft*, by H.P. Lovecraft. New York: Del Rey, 1982.

De Camp, L. Sprague. Lovecraft: A Biography. New York: Doubleday, 1975.

Caywood, Carolyn. "The Book Whose Reputation Preceded It." *School Library Journal*, Vol. 39, Issue 11, Nov. 1993.

Conover, Willis, and H.P. Lovecraft. *Lovecraft at Last*. Arlington, VA: Carrollton-Clark, 1975.

_____. "How Bad Are Lovecraft's Revisions?" *The Scream Factory*. Scottsdale: Deadline Publications, 1990.

Lovecraft, Howard Phillips. *The Annotated H.P. Lovecraft*. Ed. S.T. Joshi, New York: Dell Publishing, 1997.

_____. *The Best of H.P. Lovecraft*. New York: Del Rey, 1982.

_____. *The Call of Cthulhu and Other Stories*. Ed. S.T. Joshi. New York: Penguin, 1999.

_____. *The Dream Cycle of H.P. Lovecraft*. New York: Del Rey, 1995.

_____. *Lord of a Visible World: An Autobiography in Letters*. Ed. S.T Joshi and David E. Schultz. Athens: Ohio University Press, 2000.

_____. *The Lurking Fear and Other Stories* (a.k.a. *Cry Horror!*). New York: Avon Books, 1947.

_____. *Selected Letters: 1911-1924*. Ed. August Derleth and Douglas Wandrei. Sauk City, Wisc.: Arkham House, 1965.

_____. *Selected Letters: 1925-1929*. Ed. August Derleth and Douglas Wandrei. Sauk City, Wisc.: Arkham House, 1965.

_____. *Selected Letters: 1929-1931*. Ed. August Derleth and Douglas Wandrei. Sauk City, Wisc.: Arkham House, 1965.

_____. *Selected Letters: 1932-1934*. Ed. August Derleth and J. Turner. Sauk City, Wisc.: Arkham House, 1965.

_____. *Selected Letters: 1934-1937*. Ed. Derleth, August, and J. Turner. Sauk City, Wisc.: Arkham House, 1965.

_____. *Supernatural Horror in Literature*. New York: Ben Abramson, 1945.

_____. *The Tomb*. New York: Ballantine, 1970.

_____. *The Transition of H.P. Lovecraft*. New York: Del Rey, 1996.

Schoell, William. Afterword to *The Dragon*. New York: Leisure, 1989.

_____. "Hidden Horrors." *The Scream Factory*. Scottsdale: Deadline Publications, 1990.

_____. "Pickman's Children." *2 AM Magazine*, 1992.

Websites

The H.P. Lovecraft Archive: http://www.hplovecraft.com/
H.P. Lovecraft Library: http://www.gizmology.net/lovecraft/
The Works of H.P. Lovecraft: http://www.dagonbytes.com/thelibrary/lovecraft/

Index